Masters of cinema

Roman Polanski

David Ehrenstein

Mia Farrow in *Rosemary's Baby* (1968).

Contents

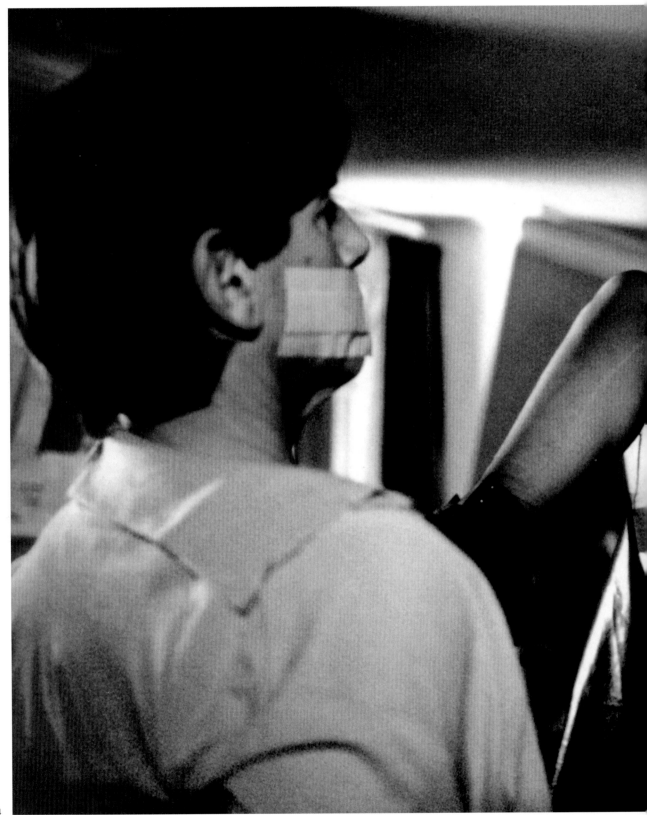

Introduction

Roman Polanski. The name is synonymous with cinema and scandal. You don't have to be an inveterate moviegoer to be familiar with *Rosemary's Baby* and *Chinatown*. And if you are aware of the length and breadth of Polanski's career, then you know that these films are just two of its many high points. For Roman Polanski has made his mark as distinctively as Alfred Hitchcock and Luis Buñuel.

Polanski has had an unusual life. His mother was taken off to a Nazi concentration camp and exterminated on arrival — a fact he didn't learn until years afterward. Escaping the ghetto and out of contact with his father, Polanski spent his childhood on the run, passing himself off as a gentile orphan, living with whatever families would give him shelter, getting whatever he could in the way of education. Later, his wife Sharon Tate was murdered by the psychotic Charles Manson's "family." And then there was his ill-advised dalliance with an underage would-be actress.

Yet, though he has witnessed horrors beyond our wildest imaginings, Polanski has made a kind of peace with them through his art. This can be seen in one of his earliest cinematic stirrings, *A Murderer*, made as his "audition" for the National Film School in Lodz, where he learned his basic craft. Only one minute and twenty-seven seconds long, *A Murderer* begins with a close-up of a door handle. The handle turns, the door opens, and a figure in a black coat comes through and walks across what we can now see is a bedroom. There's a shirtless man asleep on a bed. The intruder takes out a knife and stabs him. After turning to reveal his grinning face, he leaves the room, shutting the door behind him.

The film is too brief to be a "cautionary tale," or a "character study." It simply shows Death's arrival "like a thief in the night," murderous violence in its very essence: it's swift, unsubtle, we can't anticipate it, and there's nothing we can do about it. In other words, *A Murderer* takes us to the terrifying place Polanski has lived in for the better part of his life — and leaves us there. And it demonstrates precisely why he is a *Master of cinema*.

Peter Coyote and Emmanuelle Seigner in *Bitter Moon* (1992).

Playing with knives

Knife in the Water, Repulsion

Roman Polanski with Catherine
Deneuve in January 1966.

Brilliant beginnings

"The culmination of my first New York visit," Polanski writes in his memoir[1], "came when a still from *Knife in the Water* appeared on the cover of the September 20, 1963, issue of *Time* ... I knew of course that *Time* was an important magazine, but my main impression had been of its traditional covers—those old-fashioned portraits of public figures that *Time* editors then favored. Running a black and white still from an Eastern European movie was a daring innovation which I was unable to appreciate."

While "Cinema as an International Art" emblazoned *Time*'s cover, the story inside was entitled "Cinema: A Religion of Film." This was entirely appropriate for Polanski, who had treasured whatever films he could manage to see while living his life on the run. Laurence Olivier's *Hamlet* (1948) and Carol Reed's *Odd Man Out* (1947) made particular impressions on him—the former for its stylish acting, the latter for its study of an IRA fugitive in desperate circumstances that mirrored his own. For, from the very first, the world he lived in was one in which he never knew whom he could trust.

Though its story bears no resemblance to these classics, *Knife in the Water* (1962) has traces of both in its style. It brought Polanski into their circle. For the *Time* cover jump-started Polanski's career on a scale of which most people would only daydream. Here was *Time* saying not only that *Knife in the Water* was a "must-see" movie, but also that it was one that represented "Cinema as an International Art."

The fact of the matter is *Time* wasn't being hyperbolic. This was a director no one had ever heard of, from a country whose cinematic offerings had never cracked the "art house" ceiling, yet he had made something equal to those the finest established European talents (Fellini, Antonioni, Bergman) were producing at that very moment. *Knife in the Water* was a perfect choice for screening at New York's soon-to-be-prestigious Film Festival, whose premiere slate of offerings included Alain Resnais' *Muriel*, Joseph Losey's *The Servant*, and Yasujiro Ozu's *An Autumn Afternoon*. Like them, *Knife in the Water* has a small cast and a simple narrative unfolding in a circumscribed setting. Add sexual tension and you have yourself a "crossover" hit. For while *Knife in the Water* was a foreign-language film, its story and characters had international appeal. Even more striking was the fact that it wasn't made in France or Italy but, of all places, Poland.

"Cinema: A Religion of Film"

During the summer of 1963 Polanski went to New York to promote his first feature film, Knife in the Water. *The film appeared on* Time*'s cover, and the magazine dedicated an article to it.*

It wasn't the sort of place people usually see a movie in. No boorish Moorish architecture, no chewing gum under the seats. Instead the hall was a deep blue nave, immensely high and still, looped gracefully with golden galleries. And the images on the screen were not the sort one sees at the average alhambra. No Tammy, no Debbie, no winning of the West. Instead, a bear roamed and roared in a Mexican mansion [*The Exterminating Angel*], a regiment of French actors fought the American Civil War [*In the Midst of Life*] and a samurai disemboweled himself right there in front of everybody [*Hara-kiri*]. The first New York Film Festival now at Lincoln Center's Philharmonic Hall ... *Knife in the Water* is a Polish thriller as sharp as a knife and as smooth as water. Director Roman Polanski, 30, puts two lusty men and one busty woman aboard a small sailboat, throws them a knife, and for the next 90 minutes lets the tension build, build, build.

This is an extract from "Cinema: A Religion of Film," *Time* magazine, September 20, 1963.

Left: Zygmunt Malanowicz, Jolanta Umecka and Leon Niemczyk in *Knife in the Water* (1962).

Jolanta Umecka and Leon Niemczyk in *Knife in the Water* (1962).

A couple with issues

Wasn't Poland supposed to be a communist country? And didn't that mean a land of dour collective farms and dowdy factories? So where did this couple—he in his crisp white suit, she in her chic spectacles, fit in? Had we been lied to by our famously "free press"? Had we been provided with only superficial overviews and "received wisdom," rather than the more complex and nuanced picture of Poland we see here? It would appear so. The film's couple, Andrzej (Leon Niemczyk) and Krystyna (Jolanta Umecka), would be totally recognizable in France, England or the United States. And so, too, would the unnamed drifter (Zygmunt Malanowicz) who, having hitched a ride with them in their car, goes sailing with them as well—at Andrzej's express invitation.

It's clear that this couple "have issues." And it's likewise apparent that this sexy drifter is going to bring them to a boil. *L'Avventura* (1960) had also dealt with romantic dissatisfaction and sexual betrayal on a sailing vacation. But the boat in *Knife in the Water* is much smaller and less populated than

Zygmunt Malanowicz and Jolanta Umecka in *Knife in the Water* (1962).

the lavish yacht in Antonioni's film. And though the concerns of its passengers are much the same, Polanski declines to pitch them in an "epic" key. Like *L'Avventura*, *Knife in the Water* might be called a study in "alienation." Still, there's no real "back-story" for these characters.

We sense trouble between husband and wife right from the start. The hitchhiker has no particular "agenda." He doesn't make an immediate play for our anti-heroine. Obviously the sight of her lying on the ship's deck and taking the sun is provocative. Yet Polanski frames her in a cool, almost painterly, manner that's part of the film's compositional strategy. Likewise, Polanski perches his camera at the top of the ship's mast, taking in the characters and sea from a God-like perspective. But there is no God here, only mortals playing games with one another, beginning with a round of pick-up sticks and escalating to a tussle between the men over a knife.

As critic Raymond Durgnat notes, "Devious and persistent as it is, the antagonism of generations is compounded by a class antagonism which is no less complex. We hardly know whether the boy's general deprivation is the product of a subtle but obstinate proletarian under-privilege, persisting despite communism, or whether his sullenness is that of a student, semi-dropout, or whether he represents some admixture of the two attitudes—an admixture subsequently conspicuous in the West."[2] Whatever the cause, the knife falls overboard—thus literalizing the film's title. Moreover, in the struggle with Andrzej, the hitchhiker falls overboard too, and vanishes.

With unrestrained anger, Krystyna calls Andrzej a murderer. Humiliated and at a loss at what to do, he swims off to report the disappearance to the police. This gives the hitchhiker, who has been hiding behind a nearby buoy, the opportunity to swim back to the boat and commingle with Krystyna, who speaks to him in an almost maternal tone about what his life as a student must be like. Naturally they make love more tenderly than we might have expected.

The boat sails back to port, the hitchhiker leaving before it's reached. Andrzej is there, saying nothing to Krystyna about the situation. They drive off in their car, coming to a crossroads where a sign indicates that a police station is nearby. He says the death must be reported. She says nothing. The last shot of the film is of the car still at that crossroads. Again, *L'Avventura* comes to mind. But at the close of that film the alienated couple look to a horizon dominated by a blank wall—and she is able to make a compassionate gesture toward her imperfect mate. Not in Polanski's world.

Swinging London

That world quickly altered, as what would come to be known as "Swinging London" was just getting underway. This was "where the action was" in the 1960s—and action was what Polanski wanted more than anything. And he got it with *Repulsion* (1965). Indicative of his resourcefulness, he chose as his producing partner Compton Films, a small company specializing in soft-core erotica rather than a major British firm. As a result, he had minimum interference and maximum flexibility in making a psychological thriller only five years after *Peeping Tom* had been so negatively received as to send its maker Michael Powell packing, taking refuge in Australia.

Polanski's London-based film is headlined by a non-native, Catherine Deneuve (Carole), who had just attained world fame in Jacques Demy's *The Umbrellas of Cherbourg*. Blonde, trim, and incredibly refined, Deneuve was the embodiment of the French feminine ideal. In fact, so perfectly did she

Catherine Deneuve in *Repulsion* (1965).

"What I like to see and what I like to make", by Roman Polanski

In 1966, Michel Delahaye and Jean-André Fieschi interviewed Roman Polanski for Cahiers du cinéma.

It seems that there is more of a relationship between *When An Angel Falls* and *Repulsion* than there is between those films and your other films. Are you conscious of that or not? And does that relate to something?

Yes, I am very conscious of that. But I don't know what that relates to. I only know there are two things in me. On the one hand, I am very sentimental, romantic, baroque; on the other, I am very rigorous. And when I make a film I discipline myself a great deal. There are lots of ideas that pass through my mind and that I force myself to reject in the name of discipline. That's also true of the work I was doing before cinema: what I was painting, drawing, etc. was very dry, very rigorous. When I was filming *Two Men and A Wardrobe* I tried my best to keep within the bounds of a certain form that I believe proper to the short film. Strictly without dialogue. I believe that dialogue doesn't really fit the short film. It is purely out of habit that people put it in. In fact, when you hear people speaking in a short, this suggests that it might be a feature film, and actually you expect it to last more than the usual twenty minutes. So, I forced myself to make a short film that would be truly short, therefore removing anything that would belong to the spirit of a feature film.

But when you have restricted yourself to a strict form for some time, you feel like freeing yourself. If only to try another set of rules. As for myself, I had an urge to let my films talk, and also for as long as I wished... At the same time, my natural inclination, which is baroque, requires that I give it a free field sometimes. Thus, *When An Angel Falls* corresponds more to my nature than to my strict way of working. And that corresponds, too, more to what I like to *see* in filmmaking than to what I like to *make* myself.

In any case, I love cinema. I love watching horror films, westerns. I like to be afraid, to laugh, to cry or to be moved. I like all shows, including magic and conjuring tricks. So, I adore all that but I do not make it. As I feel the need to control myself, I make something different from what I would like to see.

Thus one can say that *Knife in the Water* is more what I like to make, having forced myself to make it, while *Repulsion* is more on the side of what I like to watch. All the same, obviously I had to control myself to make it—I didn't want to end up making, using any kind of method, any kind of horror film.

Also, it is normal that I would be tempted to go in the direction of what I like to watch. When you see something that you really like, you're bound to want to do that too. When I saw *The Nutty Professor* [Jerry Lewis, 1963], I said to myself that I would love to make a film like that. But I know I never will.

This is an extract from Michel Delahaye and Jean-André Fieschi, "Paysage d'un cerveau: entretien avec Roman Polanski" ("Landscape of a Mind: Interview with Roman Polanski"), *Cahiers du cinéma*, 175, February 1966.

Roman Polanski with Catherine Deneuve on the set of *Repulsion* (1965).

Catherine Deneuve
and Patrick Wymark
in *Repulsion* (1965).

Opposite page: Catherine
Deneuve in *Repulsion* (1965).

fit this image that for over a decade she was thought
of less as an actress than a mannequin—a living
prop sophisticated talents like Buñuel and Truffaut
could use for their own, sardonic, purposes. Not
until Deneuve reached middle age did critics begin
to notice her talent. Polanski knew she was a great
actress right from the start. And this general atti-
tude is echoed in the film's narrative. For, just as
many had failed to appreciate Deneuve, so the cast
of *Repulsion*'s London overlooks the fact that her
character, Carole, is coming apart at the seams.

Hallucinations

Polanski immediately brings us right into the girl's
mental state. She's a beautician's assistant. It's an

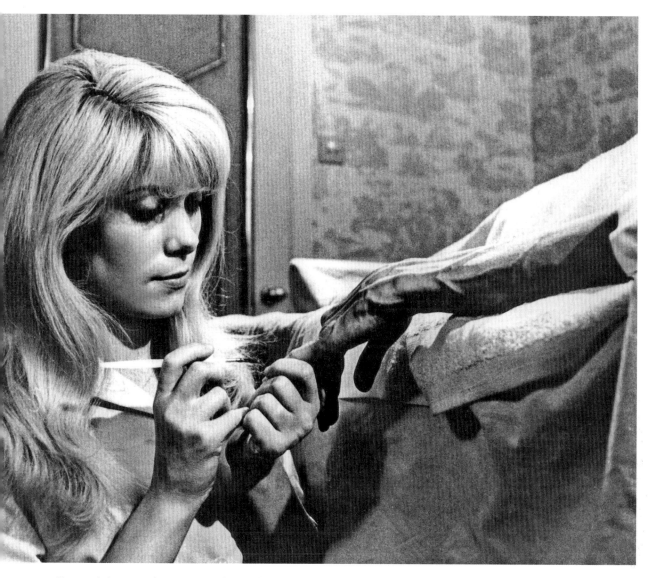

ordinary job, yet what we see through her eyes is anything but. A close-up shows a youthful hand holding a elderly one. Then we see a woman, her face covered in beauty cream, lying wrapped in a towel upon a table. We could well be in a mortuary with a corpse being prepared for funeral viewing. For this is precisely how our anti-heroine (the younger hand) feels about her job. It's as if she were attending to the living dead.

The salon Polanski used to shoot this scene belonged to Vidal Sassoon, the hair stylist central to "Swinging London." Carole's older sister Helen (Yvonne Furneaux) is definitely up for swinging. Yet, for all her smarts, Helen regards Carole's depressive state as mere moodiness. She's so busy

making plans to go on vacation with her boyfriend (Ian Hendry) that she leaves a skinned uncooked rabbit for Carole to make her own dinner, as she and the boyfriend go off without her.

Helen's not alone in this casual disregard. A nice-looking, business-suited type (John Fraser) is hot to make Carole his latest adulterous conquest. He takes no notice of her staring vacantly at a plate of unappetizing food at lunch. That lunch echoes the skinned rabbit—whose rotting head Carole has stuffed in her handbag.

As she walks down the street, a workman makes the sort of casually vulgar remark to Carole that would be ignored by most women. Polanski stages the scene as if it were something like a prelude to rape. And indeed it is for Carole, for in later scenes where she's completely alone in the apartment, she sees this workman suddenly turning up out of nowhere and attacking her. It's an hallucination. So too, obviously, are the hands she sees groping at her from the apartment's walls. Yet she's oblivious to an automobile accident she passes by in the street.

Thus the scene is set for when the would-be boyfriend drops by and she almost casually bludgeons him to death with a candelabra. It's as shocking as the murder of Marion Crane in *Psycho*. That was unexpected. This killing isn't. *Psycho*'s was protracted. This one is over in a flash. Hitchcock's setting is a classic *Old Dark House*—with an incongruously modern motel court in front of it. The apartment in *Repulsion* is perfectly ordinary. What makes it frightening are Carole's hallucinations and the extreme wide-angle lenses Polanski has cinematographer Gilbert Taylor use to depict them.

But the real horror is Carole, who looks as innocent and helpless as Lillian Gish. Hence the audience is put in the curious position of fearing for her safety—even though she's a homicidal maniac.

When Carole's sister and her boyfriend finally return there's no real sense of relief. A crowd that has been attracted to the scene gawks at the corpses (which now include the lecherous landlord) as if this was the scene of a traffic accident. Carole, now unconscious, is carried away from the scene of the crime as if she were one of its victims. And that, rather than the last shot of a family photo in which a younger and already distracted Carole appears, is the film's real payoff. For Polanski has created a heroine who is her own villain. And in this simple masterstroke has set a place apart for himself in the cinema of psychopathology.

The knife has left the water. Now it's in the flesh to stay.

Childhood memories, by Roman Polanski

I started school. It was just around the corner, and I didn't like it. School meant sitting in rows and filling up exercise books with *Ala ma kota* ("Ala has a cat"). I don't think I got much farther than that because after I was enrolled for only a few weeks, Jewish children were suddenly forbidden to attend. That was all right with me because the tedium of it all would have been unendurable except for a gadget the teacher sometimes produced. This was an epidiascope used for projecting illustrations onto a screen in the school hall. I wasn't at all interested in the words or even the pictures it projected, only in the method of projection. I wanted to know how the gadget worked and constantly examined its lens and mirror or held up the proceedings and made a nuisance of myself by masking the beam with my fingers.

I also found I could draw: not the usual childish scrawls but quite sophisticated drawings with a semblance of perspective. The portraits I made of my family were recognizable. I also remember sketching a pretty good likeness of a German soldier in his teutonic helmet. The only thing I wasn't able to copy, for some reason, was one particular Star of David. The two triangles that made up the star were interlaced with great complexity. I had plenty of time to study this pattern, however. From December 1, 1939, onward, my family had to wear strange white armbands with the Star stenciled on them in blue. I was told it meant we were Jewish.

My parents had never practiced their religion. My mother was only part Jewish, and both she and my father were agnostics who didn't believe in religious instruction for children. Now, being Jewish meant that we couldn't stay where we were. We moved yet again—not voluntarily, as at the outbreak of war, but under compulsion. We didn't have to move far. Our resettlement, which proceeded without fuss or threats, was handled by the Krakow municipal authorities, not by the Germans. Though permitted to take only as much as we could carry, we found our new quarters no worse than the old except for overcrowding. Our allocated ground-floor apartment, on Podgorze Square, on the far side of the Vistula, was bigger than my grandmother's but shared by several families. Granny was no longer with us. She had been assigned a diminutive room at the other end of Krakow's new "Jewish area."

This is an extract from Roman Polanski, *Roman by Polanski*, William Morrow and Company, New York, 1984, pp. 22–3.

Opposite page: Catherine Deneuve in *Repulsion* (1965).

Roman Polanski around 1946.

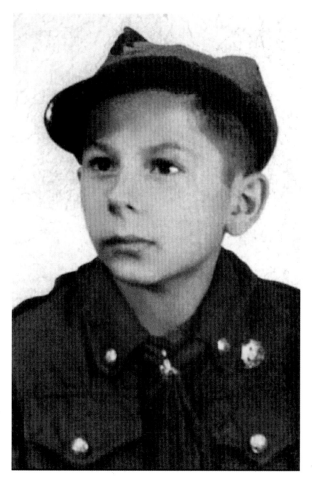

The dark fantastic

Dance of the Vampires, Rosemary's Baby, The Ninth Gate

Sharon Tate and Terry Downes
in *Dance of the Vampires* (1967).

Celluloid fantasies

"I like all horror films. They make me laugh like crazy," Polanski quipped to *Cahiers du cinéma* in 1966, citing *Peeping Tom* and *The Haunting* (Robert Wise, 1963) as particular favorites.[3] Why would a man who had witnessed so much genuine horror in actual life be so enamored of ersatz abjection? Clearly he found in celluloid fantasy a way of dealing with the residual pain of concrete reality. Perhaps what he'd seen in the Krakow ghetto and dodging the Nazis while hiding in small towns in Poland and France—running for his life—sharpened and heightened the sense of the absurd that has always marked his art. Polanski has never been given to "explanations" of his psyche or special pleading for his behavior. But the high regard in which he holds the Powell and Wise works come as no surprise to anyone familiar with Polanski's brand of the cinematically horrific, particularly *Dance of the Vampires* (1967), *Rosemary's Baby* (1968), and *The Ninth Gate* (1999). Yes, they're genre movies, but just beneath they're something more. For in very different ways this trio are thoroughgoing explorations of the terror, anxiety, and, above all, ambivalence we have about the sinister, the occult, and the "unknown."

"Parody was never my intention"

Dance of the Vampires (better known in the US by its later title, *The Fearless Vampire Killers*) began not with a story, but a setting. "Skiing down the serenely impressive Arlberg valley," Polanski recalls in an interview with the horror fanzine *Little Shoppe of Horrors*, "I realized what the setting for a picture of this type should be: not a tatty rural location situated conveniently near a film studio … but swaths of frosted pine trees, massive snowdrifts, and majestic mountain peaks."[4]

Right off the bat (to mix a metaphor), Polanski is offering innovation. Count Orlok, the cinema's first vampire, played by Max Schreck in F. W. Murnau's *Nosferatu* (1922) appears to be more rat than human. One can scarcely imagine him on skis. Likewise, Bela Lugosi in Tod Browning's *Dracula* (1931) is a creature of London's fogs. Moreover, Lugosi, swathed in a black cape, peering at the world with glowing, piecing eyes, plays the vampire as something of a "lounge lizard." Kissing Madame's hand is, of course, an appetizer for biting into her throat. The result—"living death"—is scarcely desirable, but at the last it's more discomforting than truly terrifying, at least by today's standards. These were set in 1958 by

Dracula (known as *Horror of Dracula* in the US), produced by Hammer studios, the British film production company that relaunched the gothic horror genre in the 1950s. This radical break with vampires past presented a count who wasn't a member of "polite society" but rather a denizen of dark castles and dank tombs. However, as enacted with overwhelming authority by Christopher Lee, Dracula is neither rat nor "lizard" but very much a man. Tall, thin, physically powerful, and highly sexual, he disregards the hand and goes straight for the throat—ogling milady's heaving bosom all the while.

"Parody was never my intention," Polanski told *Cahiers du cinéma*. "I wanted to make a fairy tale, something that's frightening as well as fun, but also an adventure story."[5] And indeed that's what *Dance of the Vampires* is.

Texan-born beauty

Professor Abronsius (Jack MacGowran), vampire expert, and his faithful acolyte Alfred (Polanski) venturing into the snowy regions of Transylvania, and quickly coming face to face with aristocratic bloodsucker Count von Krolock (Ferdy Mayne), is both comic *and* adventurous. Romance robustly enters the picture as Alfred falls in love with Sarah (Sharon Tate), the beautiful daughter of Shagal (Alfie Bass), the local innkeeper in the town terrorized by von Krolock's rule. Interestingly, Polanski's first choice for the role of Sarah wasn't Tate but Tuesday Weld.

That most elusively offbeat of actresses was under contract to Polanski's American co-producer Martin Ransohoff back then. A powerful force in Hollywood, Ransohoff first made his mark with the culturally reviled but incredibly popular TV sitcom *The Beverly Hillbillies* (1962—71). Then on the big

Opposite page: Roman Polanski
and Ferdy Mayne in *Dance of the
Vampires* (1967).

Below: Roman Polanski and Jack
MacGowran in *Dance of the
Vampires* (1967).

screen he changed course with such serious fare as *The Americanization of Emily* (1964) and *The Cincinnati Kid* (1965). Weld was one of the featured players of that Steve McQueen-starred drama. However, instead of her, Ransohoff offered Polanski Sharon Tate—a Texas-born beauty he had put under contract after her appearances in small TV parts and who had just been given a leading role in the occult thriller *Eye of the Devil* (1966). Polanski claimed he wasn't convinced she was up to the part of a Jewish innkeeper's daughter—until he saw her in a red wig. That may well have been true, but the finished film looks to have been conceived entirely with Tate in mind. For, as the apple of Alfred's eye and the beating heart of Count von Krolock's lust, Tate appears both semi-nude—thanks to her character's penchant for taking baths—and beautifully costumed for the vampires' ball at the film's climax. Working on a far grander scale than ever before—on locations in Italy, as well as studio-built sets in the UK—Polanski was in movie heaven. But then he was in as much bliss when the cameras were off as when they were on, for he'd fallen in love with his leading lady. Polanski and Tate instantly became Swinging London's most glamorous couple. Their happiness is clearly reflected in the tenderness with which Polanski's Alfred regards Sarah, and the way cinematographer Douglas Slocombe's camera caresses her face and form.

Jack MacGowran, Roman Polanski and Fiona Lewis in *Dances of the Vampires* (1967).

Sharon Tate: the doomed starlet

Born in Dallas, Texas, in 1943, Sharon Tate was the eldest of three daughters born to Colonel Paul Tate and his wife Doris, winning the "Miss Tiny Tot of Dallas Pageant" that year, "Miss Richland" in 1959, and " Miss Washington" in 1960. Although she spoke of an ambition to study psychiatry, it was plain that modeling and acting were in store for her. Producer Martin Ransohoff put her under contract. This led to brief "walk-on" parts in television. Then came *Eye of The Devil* (1966), a supernatural thriller starring David Niven and Deborah Kerr, and *Don't Make Waves* (1967), a comedy about Venice (California)'s "Muscle Beach."

It was during this time that Tate met Roman Polanski and won the female lead in his *Dance of the Vampires* (1967). This professional relationship rapidly developed into a personal one. They were married on January 20, 1968. While *Dance of the Vampires* (later released as *The Fearless Vampire Killers* in the US) met with only spotty commercial success, Tate went on to her most iconic commercial role as the doomed starlet in *Valley of the Dolls* (1967).

On August 8, 1969, after dinner at her favorite LA restaurant El Coyote, Tate and her friends returned to the home she and Polanski had rented from music impresario Terry Melcher at 10050 Cielo Drive in the Benedict Canyon area of Los Angeles. Polanski was in Europe, at the time, making plans for future films. With Tate at the house were Jay Sebring, celebrity hairdresser and former boyfriend of Tate, who the Polanskis had come to treasure, along with Wojciech Frykowski, an old friend of Polanski's (he had had a small acting role in *Mammals*), and his girlfriend Abigail Folger (heiress to the Folger coffee fortune). In the morning, housekeeper Winifred Chapman found them all knifed to death. The coroner's report noted that Tate was stabbed sixteen times and that "five of the wounds were in and of themselves fatal."

There is no question that had she lived, Sharon Tate would have become something other than what she is today—the most famous Hollywood murder victim next to Elizabeth Short, the so-called "Black Dahlia." You can see her potential in *Dance of the Vampires*. And with it you can feel some, though surely nowhere near all, of Polanski's pain and grief.

Opposite page: Sharon Tate and Roman Polanski in *Dances of the Vampires* (1967).

Above: Sharon Tate (on the right) in *Dances of the Vampires* (1967).

Horror and comedy

Obviously, the man who unleashed *The Beverly Hillbillies* on an unsuspecting world wasn't one for subtlety. So *Dance of the Vampires* became *The Fearless Vampire Killers*. No real damage there, but then Ransohoff added *Or Pardon Me But Your Teeth Are in My Neck*. Worse, a silly cartoon prologue was slapped onto the opening credits, "explaining" the plot and stepping on many of Polanski's carefully prepared gags. Adding insult to injury, Ransohoff ordered that several of the actors—principally Jack MacGowran—be dubbed, the better to sound more "American." And then there was the cutting of the film's original 118 minutes to 108—and in some prints less.

No wholesale slashing was done in order to accomplish this. Rather, relatively small snips were made overall to "speed things up." And this was accomplished by none other than Margaret Booth, the legendary MGM editor whose career had begun with D. W. Griffith, but whose most infamous achievement was the re-editing of John Huston's *The Red Badge of Courage* (1951), which, as outlined in *New Yorker* journalist Lillian Ross's great "inside Hollywood" report, *Picture*,[6] carved the heart out of Huston the better to make his stark anti-war drama more palatable to MGM chief Louis B. Mayer. What

Booth did to *Dance of the Vampires* wasn't so severe, but lost in her efforts was much of the atmosphere Polanski had worked to create. For, while the film is a comedy, it's a real horror film too. When Ferdy Mayne's Count von Krolock flashes his fangs, the laughter stops. Fascinatingly, this sudden jolt of horror doesn't upend the film's comedy, which is as subtle as it is broad.

A bigger thing

Although *Dance of the Vampires* ends with the announcement of the imminent arrival of the reign of vampires throughout the world, it doesn't succeed in achieving this goal itself. Polanski's version played fairly well in Europe, but in the US, the Ransohoff cut opened in only a handful of theaters. Most moviegoers didn't discover the film until several years later—after Polanski had achieved one of his greatest triumphs. However, Polanski's efforts were not in vain, for Hollywood took notice and he was on his way to bigger things.

The first of them was to have been *Downhill Racer,* a skiing story that Paramount wanted for Robert Redford. Studio chief Robert Evans sent Polanski the script. But along with it he included an advance copy of a thriller that was about to be published and that Paramount was keen on: *Rosemary's Baby*. Polanski put down *Downhill Racer* and sat up all night reading Ira Levin's novel instead.

As critic Andrew Sarris noted, Levin (the creator of such clever bestsellers as *The Boys from Brazil* and *The Stepford Wives*) had produced "a plot so effectively original that it is deserving more of a patent than a copyright."[7] In telling the story of a sweet childlike young woman married to a voraciously ambitious actor who, the better to advance his career, offers his wife's body to a devil-worshipping cult in order to be impregnated by Old Nick himself, Levin managed to make something totally outrageous utterly compelling. In bringing this to the screen Polanski ups the ante by shooting in a very real New York, and populating the supporting cast with a host of well-seasoned character actors (among them, Ruth Gordon, Sidney Blackmer, Patsy Kelly, and Ralph Bellamy) to play a clutch of devil-worshippers far closer to a West Side coffee klatch than a Satanic coven.

Mia Farrow in *Rosemary's Baby* (1968).

A waking nightmare
Rosemary's Baby

Dream sequences are nothing new to European cinema. Ingmar Bergman's *Wild Strawberries* (1957) and Federico Fellini's *8½* (1963) contain two of the most famous ones. But in Hollywood, outside of a brief vogue in the 1940s, inspired by popular interpretations of Freudian psychoanalysis (*Spellbound, Flesh and Fantasy*), dream sequences rarely featured in films aimed at a mass audience. And certainly not ones like that in *Rosemary's Baby*. In order to anaesthetize the heroine in preparation for Satanic impregnation, wily witch Minnie Castevet has given Rosemary a drug-laden dessert to eat. But Rosemary, realizing it tastes funny, eats only a few spoonfuls of the chocolate mousse—which Minnie insists on calling "mouse"—before throwing it away without Guy (her husband), who has insisted she finish it, noticing. What she's eaten is strong enough to make her dazed, but not so strong as to render her unconscious.

She collapses while walking toward the living room to see the Pope's appearance on television. Guy puts her to bed, but the actual bedroom quickly disappears, and we see—from Rosemary's point of view—her mattress floating on the ocean. Suddenly we're on a boat. Meanwhile, in the bedroom, Guy undresses her and she finds herself first naked on the boat, then wearing her swimsuit. She sees Hutch on the dock. "Isn't Hutch coming with us?" Rosemary asks. "Catholics only," an unidentified off-screen voice replies. "I wish we weren't bound by these prejudices." And then we see her on a scaffold being raised to the ceiling of the Sistine Chapel and Michelangelo's depiction of God creating Man. Hutch, meanwhile, is found standing on a stretch of desert in a dust storm yelling "Typhoon!" Rosemary is told by a sailor on the ship to "go below." But "below" is a big, dark room, obviously somewhere inside the Bramford building.

Rosemary is on a mattress again, but this time surrounded by a crowd of naked elderly people listening to Roman, dressed in some sort of high priest's robe, leading a ceremonial chant. "She's awake. She can see us," says Guy, also naked. "She can't see. As long as she ate the mouse she's like dead. Now sing," says Minnie, naked as well. This, if we're wise to the plot, is real. Unreal is the appearance of a woman in a diaphanous white dress running down a stairway and announcing to Rosemary, who says she has been bitten by a mouse, that they should tie her up in case she has convulsions. Then it's back to reality: Guy with mud on his face climbs naked on top of Rosemary. It's then that we see a close-up of a large claw-like hand with sharp pointed nails running over the young woman's body, then a pair of red eyes blazing in darkness. "This is no dream. This is really happening!," she realizes. "They

tell me you've been bitten by a mouse," says the Pope, who holds up his ring for Rosemary to kiss. But the ring looks exactly like the amulet around Rosemary's neck. Satan is now the Pope. And Polanski has successfully executed one of the most remarkable dream sequences in film history, mixing his heroine's memories and fantasies with the terrible reality of being impregnated by Satan— truly a nightmare made real.

Mia Farrow, John Cassavetes and Michael Shillo in *Rosemary's Baby* (1968).

John Cassavetes and Mia Farrow in *Rosemary's Baby* (1968).

Once again, Polanski's first choice for the leading role was Tuesday Weld, as he saw the heroine as a healthy "All-American Girl." Paramount production chief Robert Evans, however, pushed for Mia Farrow, whose success on the *Peyton Place* television series had made her ripe for movie stardom. Farrow's seeming fragility is a world away from Weld's robustness. But after auditioning her for the part, Polanski sensed an inner toughness that would be perfect for the project. And though young, she was directly connected to the golden age of the studios: her father was hardboiled director John Farrow (*The Big Clock, Hondo*) and her mother Maureen O'Sullivan (most famous as *Tarzan*'s "Jane"), so she was "right on the same page" as all the veteran players. The sole "outsider," as it were, was John Cassavetes as Rosemary's husband Guy. He was very much part of the Method school of naturalistic performing, and a director in his own right of several much-discussed independently made dramas (*Shadows*, 1959), whose style

Polanski disliked. But he was perfect for Guy, his good looks and energy bolstering a slightly sinister aura. The third most important character was the Dakota apartment building.

Completed in 1884, this massive gothic affair on the corner of West 72nd Street and Central Park West was a fashionable *pied-à-terre* for turn-of-the-century swells. It was production designer Richard Sylbert who suggested to Polanski that he use The Dakota, with its high-peaked roofs and gingerbread wainscotting, as a stand-in for "The Bramford" of Levin's novel. And when Mia Farrow intones over the opening credits the eerie wordless lullaby created for her by composer Krzysztof Komeda, it's almost as if the building itself were singing.

Nothing sinister

Right at the start, when Rosemary and Guy are shown around by the fussy manager (played by the great Elisha Cook Jr.), who makes a point of 29

brushing a fly off the back of the elevator operator's coat, a tone of "harmless" eccentricity is set. But ambiguity also comes through when they're shown the apartment that's for rent, where the last tenant—an elderly woman who expired at a nearby hospital—had lived for many years. "There's a closet behind that secretary," the manager exclaims when he notices that a very large and imposing bookcase has been moved from the hall to block this closet door. How could this sick old woman have moved it, and above all, why? With Guy's help it's moved back. The closet door is opened to reveal—a vacuum cleaner, spare shelving, and some towels. No, nothing sinister after all.

However, as we eventually learn, Guy makes a pact with his neighbors Minnie and Roman Castevet without Rosemary knowledge: they will give Guy fame and fortune in exchange for Rosemary, who they plan to have impregnated by Satan himself. Sounds ridiculous, doesn't it? But Polanski makes

us share not only Rosemary's objective experiences, but her subjective ones as well. And, in them, she's impregnated by the Devil himself.

A scene from *Rosemary's Baby* marks Polanski's mastery—and nearly got him into trouble. Having been told by Rosemary that she's pregnant, Minnie is on the phone calling her good friend Dr. Sapirstein (Ralph Bellamy), a famous pediatrician, for an appointment. But what we see—like the shot of the cigarette smoke—is what Rosemary sees—a doorway with only part of Minnie's back visible as she sits making the call. When some Paramount executives saw this shot in the rushes they were beside themselves with distress. How could a talented director have made such a mistake? Why isn't Ruth Gordon's entire body visible? The scene would have to be re-shot. But it wasn't. For these same executives were shocked when preview audiences were seen leaning forward at an angle, as of they could somehow enter the frame and get a better view.

A fearful pregnancy,
by Andrew Sarris

In 1968, the American film critic Andrew Sarris analyzed the fear of pregnancy in Rosemary's Baby *in The Village Voice.*

Rosemary's Baby is more than just a good yarn [...] Its power to terrify readers and viewers, particularly women, derives not from any disrespect toward the Deity nor from any literal fear of embodied evil. Ghosts, Holy or unholy, have ceased to haunt our dreams in their metaphysical majesty. The devil in *Rosemary's Baby* is reduced to an unimaginative rapist performing a ridiculous ritual. It could not be otherwise in an age that proclaims God is Dead. Without God, the devil is pure camp, and his followers fugitives from a Charles Addams cartoon.

What is frightening about Rosemary's condition is her suspicion that she is being used by other people for ulterior purposes. She has no family of her own to turn to, but must rely on a husband who seems insensitive to her pain, neighbors who seem suspiciously solicitous, a doctor whose manner seems more reassuring than his medicine, and a world that seems curiously indifferent to her plight. When she tells her story to a disinterested doctor, he dismisses it as pure paranoia as most doctors would if a pregnant woman walked into their office and told them the plot of *Rosemary's Baby*. The disinterested doctor calls the witch doctor and Rosemary is delivered to her satanic destiny. After spitting in her husband's face, Rosemary approaches the rocker where her yellow-eyed baby is crying and by slowly rocking the infant to sleep acknowledges her maternal responsibility toward a being that is after all a baby and ultimately HER baby.

Thus two universal fears run through *Rosemary's Baby,* the fear of pregnancy, particularly as it consumes personality, and the fear of a deformed offspring with all the attendant moral and emotional complications. Almost any film that dealt directly with these two fears would be unbearable to watch because of the matter-of-fact clinical horror involved. By dealing obliquely with these fears, the book and the movie penetrate deeper into the subconscious of the audience. It is when we least expect to identify with fictional characters that we identify most deeply. If Levin had been fully aware of the implications of what he had been writing, he would have been too self-conscious to write it. Conversely, Polanski who is too aware of implications and overtones could never have invented the plot of *Rosemary's Baby*. Hence, the fruitful collaboration of instinct and intellect on this occasion.

This is an extract from Andrew Sarris, "Rosemary's Baby," *The Village Voice*, Vol. XIII, No. 41 (July 25, 1968).

Opposite page: Mia Farrow in *Rosemary's Baby* (1968).

Following pages: Mia Farrow in *Rosemary's Baby* (1968).

What follows are scenes that become increasingly frightening until the climatic moment when Rosemary gives birth. She's then informed that "There were complications." "I don't believe you. You're lying," she says, and they sedate her. But Rosemary, who keeps hearing a baby crying, finds it by going through the closet that connects the two apartments. There she discovers the coven and a black crepe-covered cradle. Rosemary looks in—and stifles a scream. "What have you done to his eyes?" she wails. "He has his father's eyes," Roman replies, celebrating Satan's triumph. "You don't have to join, Rosemary. Be a mother to your baby," he tells her. And so she does. Smiling, she approaches the cradle, while we hear the lullaby and the end credits roll.

But what about the baby? We never see it. Always leaving us wanting more, Polanski refuses to give us the final confirmation that would make what he has shown us not a hysterical fantasy but real. The result is a film that is both. After all what's worse: a satanic child, or a woman who thinks she's given birth to a satanic child?

A return to the satanic world

Thirty-one years after *Rosemary's Baby*, Polanski returned to satanic realms with *The Ninth Gate*. Adapted from Arturo Pérez-Reverte's 1993 novel *The Club Dumas*, Polanski's film centers on a freelance rare-book finder called Dean Corso (Johnny Depp), a name redolent of the Beat Generation. While literate, Corso is by no means scholarly—but neither is he naive like Rosemary. He tracks down books much the way a private eye looks for a "missing person." A wealthy, smug, and domineering collector named Boris Balkan (Frank Langella) has hired Corso to find *The Nine Gates of the Kingdom of Shadows*, a book published in 1666 by one Aristide Torchia, a sorcerer who the Spanish Inquisition burned alive.

Clearly Corso's mission is sinister. He takes off for Europe and we quickly come to see that 31

Balkan is using him so that he can eradicate every possible antiquarian rival. But who is the beautiful young woman (played by Emmanuelle Seigner, Mrs Polanski) who keeps showing up to help our anti-hero? In fact, at one point she is seen (by us but not Corso) flying through the air, the better to best one of Balkan's henchman who is out to eliminate our anti-hero.

At the end of the movie, the collector sets about finishing his project. The illustrations in the three copies of Torchia's book, the only ones that have survived through the centuries, form a cryptogram that properly decoded will give him untold demonic powers. One of the illustrations Balkan uses, however, proves to be a forgery. And so, having accidentally set himself and his castle on fire, Balkan burns to death. As the flames rise, Corso and the girl—obviously some kind of "Guardian Devil"— make love in the grass outside. Apparently it's no accident that the naked woman in the Torchia illustrations resembles Corso's new love. Moreover, it's clearly implied that thanks to her he's going to be able to achieve the transcendence Balkan failed at so spectacularly.

Does this imply that in the end the Prince of Darkness isn't as horrid as we've been led to believe? This question is left as wide open as the actual appearance of Satan's son in *Rosemary's Baby*. With Polanski ambiguity is all.

Johnny Depp in *The Ninth Gate* (1999).

Polanskiesque

Cul-de-Sac, What?, The Tenant, Pirates, Bitter Moon

Roman Polanski
in *The Tenant* (1976).

Dark, dislocated, and nightmarish

Serious film directors strive for styles all their own. Great directors go even further. Not content to simply execute a professional job, these *auteurs* produce works whose distinctiveness is indelible. And it's among these that we find directors whose names have spawned adjectives—Hitchcockian, Buñuelian and, most famously of all, Felliniesque. Naturally, there's also a Polanskiesque style.

What is the Polanskiesque style? It's sardonic like Buñuel, dramatic like Hitchcock, and dreamlike like Fellini. But it's also something else. For in its radical combination of the absurd, the erotic, and the uncanny, the Polanskiesque takes us to that place where nightmares become objects of desire. In short, while Polanski's films seem to begin in precise genres, they go where genre films dare not tread.

Cul-de-Sac (1966) and *Bitter Moon* (1992) are sterling examples of this. *What?* (1972), *The Tenant* (1976), and *Pirates* (1986)—striking but less commercially viable—follow the same tendencies. Their penchant for the sexually *outré* and the comically bizarre uncovers layers of meaning that can be found even in such otherwise sober Polanski works as *Death and the Maiden* (1994) and *The Pianist* (2002).

For Polanski sees the world though a prism that is dark, dislocated, and nightmarish.

A textbook case

Cul-de-Sac is a key Polanski work in this regard. At its center is a strikingly mismatched couple—George and Teresa (Donald Pleasence and Françoise Dorléac)—living in a remote castle on the island of Lindisfarne, off the coast of Northumberland. This tiny peninsula is surrounded by a large expanse of water that at high tide cuts the place off completely from the mainland. It would seem made for Polanski to shoot this bohemian domestic drama crossed with a gangsters-on-the-run thriller; a plot and setting worthy of Samuel Beckett.

George and Teresa are far more unsettled than the couple in *Knife in the Water*, but how and why they came together is a question Polanski never answers. Their tenuous marriage finally unravels with the intrusion of two gangsters, the fat Dickie (Lionel Stander) and the small Albie (Jack MacGowran). Their forerunners can be found in *The Fat and the Lean* (1961), a signal work in which a master seated in his rocking chair (André Katelbach) and his faithful slave (Polanski) are found on the terrace of a desolate house on the outskirts of Paris (the

Polanski's music

Born Krzysztof Trzci ski in 1931, "Komeda" was a stage name assumed when after six years of study this Polish Medical Academy graduate (specializing in ear, nose, throat, and neck disorders) decided to become a jazz musician. From 1956 to his untimely death in 1969 he specialized in this form both with his groups, The Komeda Sextet and The Komeda Quintet, and in his compositions for films by directors Henning Carlsen (*Hunger*, 1966), Jerzy Skolimowski (*Barrier*, 1966, *The Departure*, 1967), and above all Roman Polanski. He worked with Polanski from 1958 for the short *Two Men and A Wardrobe* right through to *Rosemary's Baby*, for which, billed as "Christopher Komeda", he created his most famous score—its signature "Lullaby" (la-la-la'd by Mia Farrow) as wedded to the film as any of its startling scenes and brilliant performances.

While his pure jazz work (his 1966 album *Astigmatic* was widely hailed as marking the emergence of a specifically European aesthetic) is reminiscent of The Modern Jazz Quartet, Komeda's film scores are very much his own—a mixture of eccentric wit and subtle moodiness with a range comparable to that of Michel Legrand—perfect for works as varied as *The Fat and the Lean*, *Knife in the Water*, *Cul-de-Sac*, and *Dance of the Vampires*.

There is no doubt Komeda's success would have continued were it not for a hematoma of the brain that resulted either from a car accident in 1968 or a set-to he had with Polish writer Marek Hlasko, who during a drunken party pushed him off an escarpment. He was in any event transported back to Poland for treatment, never regained consciousness, and died in Warsaw several months later. (It is believed that Komeda may have been treated in Poland because he did not have US medical insurance.)

Since Komeda's death, Polanski has worked with a number of different composers, but only Alexandre Desplat's score for *The Ghost Writer* comes close to the subtly elusive musical scores that were Komeda's specialty.

Lionel Stander and Françoise Dorléac in *Cul-de-sac* (1966).

Eiffel Tower appears frequently in the background), enacting a kind of dance of mutual dependency. Beckett's *Waiting for Godot* is a clear inspiration here. But Polanski's "Master" and "Slave," unlike Beckett's "Pozzo" and "Lucky," are in no way verbal. In *Cul-de-Sac*, however, they're very much so: here they are not anonymous tramps but gangsters whose latest job has gone terribly wrong. Dickie is slightly wounded; Albie gravely so. The importuned couple don't appear all that "terrorized" nor the interlopers all that "dangerous," doubtless because a hallmark of the Polanskiesque is that the potential for danger is everywhere.

Dickie sneaks in the house and surprises Teresa putting a woman's nightgown on George and giggling while she adds lipstick and eyeliner to his face, enacting a cross-dressing parody of a lesbian love scene (that they've obviously enacted before). Shortly after this, Albie dies from his injuries, and Dickie, Teresa, and George bury him. It is at this moment that something closer to farce emerges with the arrival of a new group—an older and a younger couple, plus a small boy who runs about causing upset. After they have left, Dickie decides to take the couple's white luxury car—an action that provokes George to spring to sudden life. With a gun he's filched from one of their last visitors he shoots Dickie. Stumbling about, the now-dying gangster lets loose with a round from his machine gun that fails to kill anyone but does manage to blow up the car. The owner of the gun that killed him invites Teresa to leave with him. She immediately complies. And so at the end we see George, seated alone and crying desperately, not for Teresa but for his first wife Agnes.

Are we supposed to feel sorry for him? Normally this would be a film director's primary concern. But not so with Polanski, who prefers to

Lionel Stander, Françoise Dorléac and Donald Pleasence in *Cul-de-sac* (1966).

leave us in a state of emotional suspense. The film has taken us to place of desolate isolation—and left us there.

Dirty jokes, paranoia, and family entertainment

Several of Polanski's subsequent films are purely Polanskiesque in style, with varying degrees of commercial success and critical interest. *What?*, a bizarrely *outré* sex farce made in Italy in 1972 between the decidedly serious *Macbeth* (1971) and *Chinatown* (1974), starred Marcello Mastroianni. But while he plays an important role, the most screen time is given to the film's heroine, a nubile innocent abroad named Nancy, embodied by the plucky and shapely Sydne Rome.

The scenario that Polanski and Gérard Brach concocted for her, a series of sexual scenes, each one stranger than the last, is suggestive of Christian Marquand's *Candy* (1968), Terry Southern and Mason Hoffenberg's popular prurient romp. But the images we see on screen are inspired by another source: *Little Annie Fanny*, the comic strip created by Harvey Kurtzman and Will Elder that ran sporadically from 1962 to 1988 in *Playboy* magazine.[8] Shot entirely at producer Carlo Ponti's villa, with a supporting cast including Visconti veteran Romolo Valli, it's a kind of cinematic "dirty joke." The plot is Buñuel-style *déjà vu* (Nancy finds herself repeating the same scene over and over again), with sadomasochistic humiliation (when Mastroianni isn't begging Rome to whip him, he's insisting on whipping her), and overall indulgence in its handling of themes generally considered to be "of questionable taste." A Polanskiesque work aimed at "the happy few," it met with dismissive reviews and limited release, but was doubtless made because producer Ponti saw it as a way to keep a valuable director like Polanski happy.

In *The Tenant* (1976), Polanski treads more familiar ground. Adapted from a novel by illustrator and animated filmmaker Roland Topor,[9] *The Tenant* might be described as a kind of remake of *Repulsion* (with Polanski playing the Catherine Deneuve role) combined with a dash of *Rosemary's Baby*. Like that film, it features a cast of seasoned actors (Shelley Winters, Melvyn Douglas, Jo Van

Marcello Mastroianni and
Sydne Rome in *Quoi?* (1972).

41

Roman Polanski in *The Tenant* (1946).

Fleet, Lila Kedrova, Claude Dauphin) and a plot in which paranoia predominates. But Polanski's bedeviled clerk Trelkovsky isn't a sympathetic figure like Rosemary; rather, he's a weirdo like George in *Cul-de-Sac*.

The next Polanskiesque film would appear to be entirely commercial. *Pirates* (1986) was a "passion project" that Polanski had nurtured for a long time, from well before the time when pirate films were believed to be "The Next Big Thing." Indeed, this belief took another two decades to take root: it wasn't until the *Pirates of the Caribbean* (2003 onward) that such movies caught the public's fancy—in a

way that *Pirates* didn't succeed in doing. For this tale of one-legged pirate king Captain Red (Walter Matthau) and his second-in-command, The Frog (Cris Campion), is little more than a big-budget, costumed, less inspired remake of *The Fat and the Lean*.

Realizing he was scarcely cut out for anything resembling "family entertainment," the great director put his *Pirates* miscalculation behind him with his next Polanskiesque film, the decidedly adult *Bitter Moon* (1992). Neither a critical nor an audience favorite in its time, it's a film ripe for rediscovery by audiences more adventurous than those who first saw it.

A mythical duet

For the better part of Roman Polanski's career it has been impossible to pronounce his name without following it with that of Gérard Brach, a scriptwriter as associated with the director he most famously served as I. A. L. Diamond is with Billy Wilder or Jean-Claude Carrière with Luis Buñuel. The Brach–Polanski collaboration stretches from 'La Rivière de Diamants' (the Amsterdam episode of *The World's Most Beautiful Swindles*) right on through to *Bitter Moon*. Brach also worked with Jean-Jacques Annaud (*The Bear, The Name of the Rose, The Lover*), Claude Berri (*Jean de Flo-*

rette, Manon des Sources), and Michelangelo Antonioni (*Identification of a Woman*). But it's with Polanski that he is most definitively identified.

In a way, it was an early script they wrote together, but that Polanski did not direct, that clinched this collaboration. *A Taste for Women* (1964), directed by Jean Léon, is black comedy about a clutch of chic urban cannibals with a taste (in every sense of the term) for women. It is clearly a script that Polanski and Brach enjoyed writing, giving it a lightness of touch that would probably have been missed by any other *auteur* that might have

taken up such a story (Marco Ferreri, Nagisa Oshima, Raoul Ruiz). But what links Brach to Polanski most profoundly is the former's agoraphobia. Only someone profoundly fearful of leaving his apartment could script the likes of *Repulsion* and *The Tenant*. Still, he could also imagine the open air that *Tess* breathes. But there is of course a deeper aspect to all of this, touched on in a rare interview Brach granted the *Los Angeles Times* in 1994. As he explained to journalist Laurence B. Chollet, "I'm extremely sensitive to perspective, that is my problem ... It just seems to take me, you know, sweep me

away. One day years ago, I go to the Eiffel Tower, walking underneath it. I look up and I have this awful sensation of vertigo—only in reverse. I felt like I was being sucked up! Is strange, no?"

No. In the world of Roman Polanski and Gérard Brach that isn't strange at all.

Roman Polanski with Gérard Brach on the set of *Quoi?* (1972).

Following pages: Roman Polanski on the set of *Pirates* (1986).

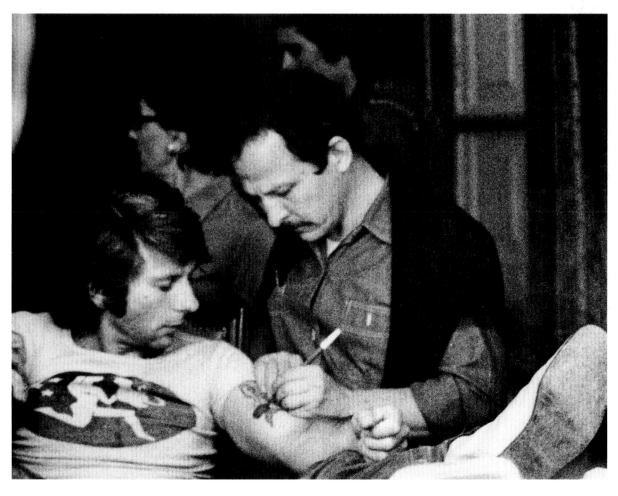

Obscure object of desire

Adapted from *Bitter Moon* (a pun on '*lune de miel*', meaning 'honeymoon') by Pascal Bruckner (a writer more famous for his diatribes against multiculturalism than his novels), this cautionary tale of *amour fou* was clearly inspired by Pierre Louÿs' *La Femme et le Patin* (*The Woman and the Puppet*, 1898), which was filmed by Josef von Sternberg as *The Devil is a Woman* (1935), Julien Duvivier as *La Femme et le Patin* (*A Woman Like Satan* in English, in 1959), and Luis Buñuel as *That Obscure Object of Desire* (1977). In each of these films, a sullen beauty captivates a man tormented by desire by making him promises, never fulfilled, of sexual union. Following in the footsteps of Marlene Dietrich, Brigitte Bardot, Carole Bouquet, and Ángela Molina, Polanski's wife Emmanuelle Seigner proceeds to drive the man wild—an easy task given her talent and beauty. The situation imagined by Bruckner enables her to play the part of temptress to an even greater extent as this

poisonous seductress is offered two new victims in addition to her husband.

It begins simply enough with a presumably happily married couple Nigel and Fiona (Hugh Grant and Kristin Scott Thomas) on a cruise ship on its way to India, with no plans to change the routine of their comfortable lives. But they meet Mimi (Emmanuelle Seigner) and her husband Oscar (Peter Coyote), a man in a wheelchair. What follows is structurally much like the scenes between Lionel Atwill's cynical aristocrat and Cesar Romero's boyish revolutionary in Sternberg's film. But in a far darker mode.

Through flashbacks, we learn how Oscar and Mimi first met. The eroticism and the violence of their relationship (she spills milk on her breasts for him to lick off, turning the movie into a sort of Bertolucci's *Last Tango in Paris*) show that, clearly, we're a long way from Sternberg, Duvivier, and Buñuel. Nigel slowly gives in to Mimi's charms while other flashbacks show us how her relationship with Oscar has gone downhill.

Then we flashback to Oscar getting struck by a car (explaining his paraplegic state) and Mimi returning to care for him. She gives him a gun as a birthday present—a clear invitation for him to commit suicide. When he doesn't take the hint, she gives him a bath and leaves him shivering in the tub while she takes a phone call. He crawls out and across the floor in one of the most cleverly sadomasochistic images in all of Polanski.

At the end of the movie, more besotted with Mimi than ever, Nigel stands on deck rehearsing what he plans to say to Fiona about how they should have an "open marriage."

That night, on the ballroom floor, Nigel dances with Mimi, declaring with utmost pathos, "I think I've fallen in love with you." "Come on. I'm just a fantasy," she says with absolute truthfulness, as Bryan Ferry's "Slave to Love" starts up in the background. But for this number the person Mimi dances with isn't Nigel but Fiona. As if in response to this climactic betrayal, a storm starts

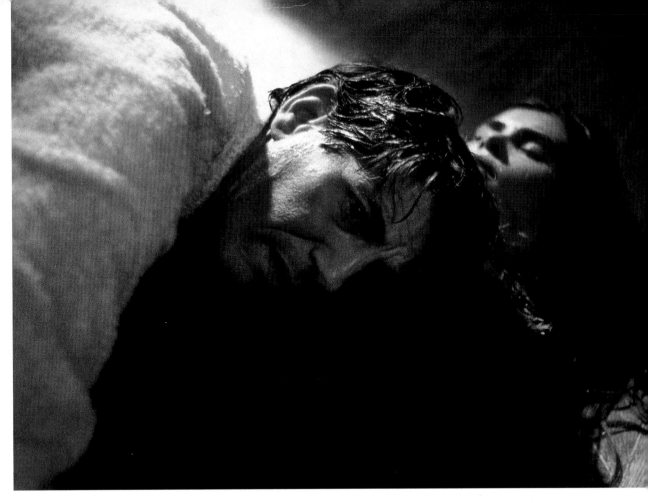

up that tosses the ship about violently. Everyone stumbles back to their cabins. When Nigel awakens in the morning, he's alone. Going to Oscar's cabin, still pathetically panting after Mimi, he finds her in bed not with Oscar but with Fiona. Oscar, who is of course present as well, laughs diabolically. Nigel, finally moved to action, tries to strangle him. Oscar pulls a gun. But his target isn't Nigel. It's Mimi— and then himself.

Are Nigel and Fiona now "sadder but wiser"? It's hard to say. At least they have no illusions, thanks to Polanski, who has changed a very real woman named Emmanuelle Seigner into a fantastic object of cinematic desire—a key construct in Polanskiesque style.

Above: Peter Coyote and Emmanuelle Seigner in *Bitter Moon* (1992).

Opposite page: Emmanuelle Seigner and Kristin Scott Thomas in *Bitter Moon* (1992).

Raymond Chandler's nightmare

Chinatown, Frantic

Jack Nicholson
in *Chinatown* (1974).

A spectacular film noir

Our story begins in 1904, the year of the Owens River Valley "Land Grab." William Mulholland, the head of the newly created Los Angeles Water Department, and Fred Eaton, LA's mayor, supposedly began searching for a new source of water for a city that was built on a desert. They found the Owens River Valley and began buying up all the pertinent land and water rights. Mulholland also conned voters into believing this acquisition was vitally important to the city, when in reality he was using much of the water to irrigate the nearby San Fernando Valley and increase the return on the investments made there by his and Eaton's friends. ,A series of bond issues promoted by Mulholland and Eaton resulted in the city buying the land from Eaton to pay for the construction of an aqueduct. Hence the residents of Owens Valley, instead of gaining a federal irrigation project as they had been led to expect, were simply exploited in order to build an aqueduct, siphoning their water to the big desert city of Los Angeles. In short, it was a perfectly legal crime.

That's what fascinated screenwriter Robert Towne when he read about it in Carey McWilliams's *Southern California Country: An Island on the Land.*[10]

And so, over half a century after the "Land Grab" took place, it was wedded to a murder-mystery plot for a film called *Chinatown*. Produced by Robert Evans, with Jack Nicholson, Faye Dunaway, and John Huston in the leading roles, this spectacular film noir has been hailed ever since as a high watermark of 1970s filmmaking and one of the crowning achievements of its director's career. Yet, as snugly as it fits into Polanski's curriculum vitae, *Chinatown* might well never have happened for him were it not for the persuasive power of Evans and Towne in getting him on board. For making *Chinatown* meant returning to Los Angeles—a city that held nothing for him save the horrific memory of the murder of his beloved wife Sharon Tate and several of their friends on August 9, 1969 by the followers of a manipulative psychotic named Charles Manson.

Evans, who as head of production at Paramount made *Rosemary's Baby* possible, was clearly in sync with Polanski's talents and sensed the power of Towne's screenplay—even though in its originally submitted form Evans claimed he didn't really understand it.[11] That's why he thought Polanski should direct the film. And he was right. Polanski saw he could work with Towne by honing the wealth of details he had amassed into a drama with a beginning, a middle and, most overwhelming of all, an end. Together they framed the historical facts that had so fascinated Towne within a crime thriller unfolding all over Los Angeles, that through the character of Huston's Noah Cross highlights the ruthless power, all-consuming ambition, and naked greed of "City Fathers" like Mulholland and Eaton.

The right kind of murder mystery

"The emotional basis of the standard detective story was and had always been that murder will out and justice will be done," wrote Raymond Chandler in the introduction to his short story collection *Trouble is My Business*.[12] "Its technical basis was the relative insignificance of everything except the final denouement. What led up to that was more or less passage work. The denouement would justify everything. The technical basis of the Black Mask [a popular pulp magazine] type of story, on the other hand, was that the scene outranked the plot, in the sense that a good plot was one that made good scenes. The ideal mystery was one you would read if the end was missing. We who tried to write it had the same point of view as the filmmakers. When I first went to Hollywood a very intelligent producer told me that you couldn't make a successful motion picture from a mystery story, because the whole point was a disclosure that took a few seconds of screen time while the audience was reaching for its hat. He was wrong, but only because he was thinking of the wrong kind of mystery."

Polanski was definitely thinking of the right kind of murder mystery. Exactly what happened to Jake Gittes (Jack Nicholson) is never said, but it's referred to by those who knew him then by a single word—which is also the film's title. Obviously what happened to Gittes in Chinatown has to do with more than vagaries of a specific LA locale. It's an abyss one peers over—and might fall into if not careful. Gittes is nothing if not careful. Consequently, he's well prepared when a woman (Diane Ladd) comes to his office, introduces herself as Mrs Evelyn Mulwray and asks him to supply proof of the affair she suspects her husband Hollis is having. Recognizing that Mulwray is the chief engineer of the Department of Water and Power, Gittes goes to a public hearing where he

sees Mulwray (Darrell Zwerling) arguing against the construction of a dam. In an image right out of Buñuel's *The Exterminating Angel* (1962), a local farmer protesting the situation brings a herd of sheep into the room.

This bit of real-life surrealism is topped by another as Jake follows Mulwray to a dry riverbed where he sees him talking to a small boy on horseback and afterward take out a large book and write in it—a book we later learn is a public record of land purchases. Jake continues to follow Mulwray to a cliff by the ocean. Night falls and Mulwray watches as water pours out of a drain in the cliff's side. What does this all mean? Impossible for either Jake or the viewer to say at this point. But so far

Jack Nicholson and Faye Dunaway in *Chinatown* (1974).

Following pages: Jack Nicholson in *Chinatown* (1974).

it's a great series of scenes in the manner Chandler approved of. Later, when Mrs Evelyn Mulwray (Faye Dunaway) appears, she is in no mood for laughing: it transpires that someone had assumed her identity to hire him and thus invade her husband's privacy. "I don't get tough with anyone, Mr Gittes. My lawyer does," she says with icy cool. When it comes to getting tough, there are precious few like Faye Dunaway. But she met her match in Polanski.

"She was a gigantic pain in the ass. She demonstrated certifiable proof of insanity," Polanski declares in his autobiography.[13] He goes on to recount an incident in which he saved time spent on her coiffure by simply pulling out a distracting hair himself. She hit the roof, but in doing so

Faye Dunaway
in *Chinatown* (1974).

let off steam that had been percolating for some time, thus "settling scores" between them—at least for a while. There was, of course, a method to this madness.

"Polanski—hardly a filmmaker dispensed toward wish fulfillment—based Evelyn's scalpeled eyebrows and gift-bow lipstick on memories of his mother, the first woman in his life to be taken from him and butchered," *Village Voice* critic Jessica Winter noted in a 2003 article on the film.[14] This wasn't the film's only personal slant. For while turning Dunaway into a mirror image of his mother (as Visconti had done with Silvana Mangano in *Death in Venice*) was making public the "private," Polanski's playing a hired thug who slashes Jake Gittes's nose with a switchblade knife cuts even deeper. This act of violence—the most extreme in the film until its grand finale—unfolds as the climax to a sequence in which Jake returns to locales Mulwray had haunted.

Mulwray's body is discovered at the Oak Canyon reservoir. But the water inside the corpse is seawater. Could it be that he was drowned in the saltwater fish pool in his home and then taken to the reservoir? Driving back to Oak Canyon, Jake is stopped by a short man in a white suit and hat saying, "Hold it there Kitty Cat," accompanied by another shady character of his acquaintance, Claude Mulvihill (Roy Jenson.) "Hey Claude, where did you get the midget?" Jake asks, as the "midget" attacks, warning him that this is what he gets for being "nosey," adding, "Next time you lose the whole thing. I'll feed it to my goldfish." Clearly here's where Polanski's assertion "I am widely regarded, I know, as an evil profligate dwarf" comes into play.[15] From this point on, the general thrust of the narrative proceeds much as in noirs past, with a romance between the detective and the good-looking widow who hides a big secret: raped by her father, Noah Cross, who is

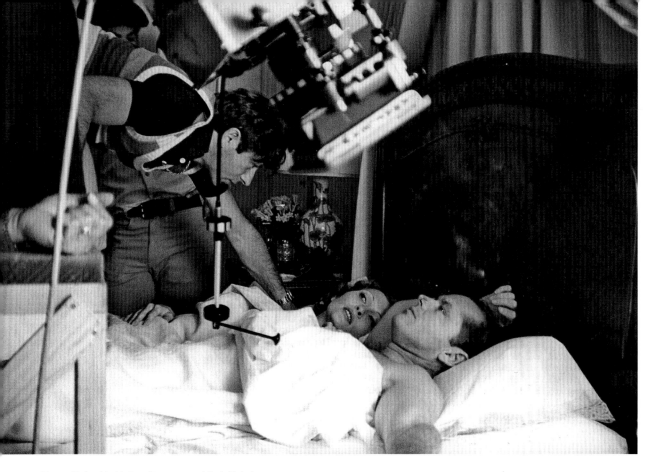

Roman Polanski with Faye Dunaway and Jack Nicholson
on the set of *Chinatown* (1974).

also her husband's associate, has a daughter who is also her sister.

At the end of the movie, Chinatown finally appears. And Evelyn, with Jake's help, is trying to make an escape with her sister—daughter. But the police, and her father, are there to stop her. "He *owns* the police," Evelyn explains as she holds her father off with a handgun, shoots at him, and misses. She rides off in the car, only to be stopped literally dead when one of the policemen fires a shot that goes right into the back of her head and through her flawed eye.

This wasn't the ending Towne wanted. A sentimental soul, he had written an escape for Evelyn and the girl. But Polanski is not a fan of happy endings, having found none in life. "I was absolutely adamant that she has to die at the end if the film has to have any meaning," Polanski said.[16] And so she did—and so it does.

What would Chandler have said? Most likely that *Chinatown* was like one of his own creations

(*The Big Sleep, The Lady in the Lake, Farewell, My Lovely, The Long Goodbye*) having a nightmare. It's a nightmare that hasn't really stopped—despite the best efforts of Towne in his Jack Nicholson-directed *Chinatown* sequel, *The Two Jakes* (1990), a simpler, well-made, but nowhere near as resonant a film. Polanski went on to move the Chandler nightmare abroad in his sleek international thriller, *Frantic* (1988).

Moving up a gear

Starring Harrison Ford as Dr Richard Walker, a blandly named, foursquare American, whose wife (Betty Buckley) is kidnapped upon their arrival in Paris, where he is attending a medical conference, *Frantic* has the cool assurance of a director ready to go a step further than Hitchcock in tales of international intrigue. That step is provided by Emmanuelle Seigner (soon to become Mrs Polanski) as Michelle, a sleekly gorgeous young woman who, while looking like a femme fatale, is as much of an innocent as our hero.

Michelle may live on the wrong side of town, have worked unknowingly as a courier for the kidnappers, and hang out in louche nightclubs frequented by *nouveaux riches* Arabs and decadent Americans, and discos where questions about a "White Lady" will lead to a dreadlocked Rastafarian selling dope, but she's a goodhearted girl nonetheless. She's much more helpful to Walker than the authorities, with their bland assurances that "We're doing all we can." Teaming up together, much as Jake and Evelyn did but without the romance, Walker and Michelle discover that what the bad guys are looking for is in a souvenir statuette of the Statue of Liberty. What's inside is far more dire than anything Jake Gittes stumbled across: it's a trigger for a portable thermonuclear device.

As in *Chinatown*, things end messily. The setup is that Walker's wife will be traded for the device. But there's a shoot-out in which the girl is killed. Although he is as upset as Jake at the end of *Chinatown*, walking off into the dark isn't Walker's style. Besides, the grand finale takes place in broad daylight. So, in revenge for all that's transpired, including the girl's death, he tosses the trigger device into the Seine. At the end, he and his wife carry the girl's body away by themselves. Hardly the Paris trip they had imagined. But this is a film by Polanski, he for whom convulsive nightmares are as common as the day is long.

58   Emmanuelle Seigner and Harrison Ford in *Frantic* (1988).

Classical Polanski

Macbeth, Tess, Oliver Twist

Jon Finch in
Macbeth (1971).

The perfect anti-hero

While Polanski has been primarily regarded as a modernist talent, he sports a highly pronounced and sophisticated classical side as well. This comes to the fore in a trio of adaptations of Shakespeare, Thomas Hardy, and Charles Dickens that may seem out of character at first glance, but on closer inspection are central to his aesthetic.

Macbeth (1971) was Polanski's first film after the Manson murders. The expectation was that the play's numerous scenes of slaughter would offer him a kind of cinematic *trauerarbeit*. But this motive is more apparent than real. Had Polanski been interested in gore alone, the rarely staged *Titus Andronicus* would have been preferable. *Macbeth* is among the Bard's most popular plays. It's tightly structured and briskly paced. Most important of all, it sports the dramatic novelty of having its hero and villain be one and the same. For Macbeth is far from a simple doer of dirty deeds. He's an intelligent man undone by ambition who is emboldened by a prophecy of ascending to the Scottish throne. Thus he is the perfect Polanski anti-hero.

While there have been many film adaptations of *Macbeth*, the two prior to Polanski's that stand out are Orson Welles's low-budget 1948 version made for Republic Pictures and Akira Kurosawa's lavish period epic *Throne of Blood* (1957), starring Toshiro Mifune and set in medieval Japan. Although there's little doubt that Polanski was well aware of both these films, his *Macbeth* might well have taken its cue from Franco Zeffirelli's *Romeo and Juliet* (1968). For just as that film cast actors closer to its protagonist's age, cueing its enormous commercial success, so does Polanski, breaking with a tradition that had the roles taken on by older and therefore presumably more "experienced" actors capable of delivering Shakespeare's speeches with proper eloquence. Jon Finch and Francesca Annis (neither major stars at the time), however, are quite up to tackling Shakespeare.

The world in which Polanski wants to set his film appears right at the start, when we see the three witches not in a cave nor before a cauldron but on a beach, burying in the sand a severed arm with a dagger in it. Two of the witches are gnarled and aged as always. But the third is strikingly young, with a pronounced resemblance to Manson "family" member Lynette "Squeaky" Fromme. Still, one must not forget *Rosemary's Baby*, the film Polanski made before the Tate—LaBianca tragedy. That featured elderly witches in modern

New York. Likewise, unproblematic for Polanski is Macbeth's "Is this a dagger which I see before me?" speech, which the director neatly illustrates with a shot of a dagger hanging in midair.

Like Noah Cross, Macbeth wants power. Still, he hesitates before murdering the king, who hauntingly calls his name before the fatal blow is struck. As in a savage rite, Macbeth, once proclaimed king, is held aloft on a shield. Similarly novel is Macbeth's premonitory dream of Banquo's child taking revenge on him, prior to Banquo's murder, and the chilling almost off-hand way in whichMacbeth's solders dispatch the killers hired to murder Banquo.

The appearance of Banquo's ghost before Macbeth at the banquet is one of the play's big moments. Characteristically, Polanski innovates. We see Banquo first as merely pale, then covered in blood, then reflected in a series of mirrors. Also noteworthy is the scene where Macbeth goes to consult with the witches again, finding himself surrounded by a mob of naked elderly people—like the ones in the impregnation scene of *Rosemary's Baby*. They give Macbeth a potion, by means of

Above: *Macbeth* (1971).

Opposite page: Peter Firth and Nastassja Kinski in *Tess* (1979).

which he sees his own reflection in water saying "Beware Macduff," which is instantly followed by the appearance of two young men dressed in white delivering the line "till Birnam Wood comes to Dunsinane."

At the time of *Macbeth*'s release, several critics commented on the sight of Lady Macbeth totally naked, unhinged, and muttering about the blood that can't be washed off. Was this the result of *Macbeth* being a *Playboy* Production? It's just a novelty, like Macbeth's "Tomorrow, and tomorrow, and tomorrow," which is at first delivered as an interior monologue, until "Out, out, brief candle! Life's but a walking shadow ..." is spoken full out. As for the grand finale, while it sports the usual swordplay, Macbeth is not simply killed but beheaded. One sees here an ability to look savagery right in the eye and proclaim Macbeth's victims no better than he is, but it also echoes the bouncing head that the psychotic protagonist of *The Tenant* sees outside his window. And yet it doesn't stop there. For before the end credits roll, Polanski takes us to the edge of the witches' lair, where we see another man of Macbeth's about to enter, the better to learn his fortune. For Polanski, murderous ambition is a constant in the human character.

Innocence undone

With *Tess* (1979), the *trauerarbeit* takes a gentler but more explicit form in that adapting Hardy's nineteenth-century novel to the screen was something that Sharon Tate herself had suggested to her husband, which is why the dedication "For Sharon" appears on the film's opening credits. Did she fancy the leading role? Perhaps. But Polanski found an ideal Tess in Nastassja Kinski. The daughter of unhinged character star Klaus Kinski, she had made a decorative debut in Wim Wenders' *The Wrong Move* (1975) but had never been given a serious role before. Polanski saw in Kinski (with whom he'd had an affair when she was fifteen) someone who could embody a role just enough, allowing him to supply the cinematic context to carry her through.

Coming as it did in the wake of Polanski's forced return to Europe as a result of the Samantha Geimer encounter, it would not be unreasonable to suspect that he saw *Tess* as an *apologia pro vita sua*. 63

Roman Polanski with Nastassja
Kinski on the set of *Tess* (1979).

As *New York Times* film critic Janet Maslin pointed out in her review, "When *Tess* was shown at the Cannes Film Festival, the press pointed nastily and repeatedly to the coincidence of Mr. Polanski's having made a film about a young girl's seduction by an older man, while he himself faced criminal charges for a similar offense."[17] But such suppositions are inappropriate. For Polanski presents Hardy's brave and resolute heroine at the mercy of the roué Alec d'Urberville (Leigh Lawson) and the prig Angel Clare (Peter Firth).

Polanski was taking more than a chance in tackling Hardy's book. The last big-screen Hardy adaptation, *Far from the Madding Crowd* (1967), was a major flop—despite the fact that director (John Schlesinger), screenwriter (Frederic Raphael), and star (Julie Christie) had just had a resounding success with *Darling* (1965). Budgeted at $12 million, *Tess* was the most expensive French film made up to that date. At three hours when first shown at Cannes, it was deemed too long for commercial success, but this objection was quickly swept aside when *Los Angeles Times* critic Charles Champlin gave the Cannes cut a rave review. Columbia Pictures elected to release *Tess* as it was. The film was an enormous hit in the US and made a star of its leading lady. For Polanski, *Tess* was both a detour and a continuation, for it dealt with innocence undone in a milder mode than he'd trafficked in before.

Passions as old as time itself

A note of expectant calm is struck right at the start, where a group of young girls, all in white, are seen dancing gaily in a field during a country festival. Tess is among them, but Polanski's camera doesn't pick her out right away. We see her in this general context before a shot arrives of her standing calmly, not drawing attention to herself. It's a key to her character. Tess instinctively *recedes*. It's her future husband, Angel Clare (Peter Firth), who stands out here—taking gentlemanly notice of the girls and speaking to them. But this pastorale gives way to something less exalted in the scenes that follow as Tess's father, John Durbeyfield (John Collin) is informed that he's a poor relative of the wealthy d'Urbervilles. And so he sends his daughter Tess off to collect the fortune he imagines to be his. What she finds instead is a suave seducer, Alec d'Urberville (Leigh Lawson), who in a scene that deftly mixes innocence and libertinage, feeds Tess fresh strawberries by hand.

Needless to say, no good comes of this. Tess soon finds herself pregnant. Proud by nature, she refuses to inform the child's father. When the baby sickens and dies, the local vicar refuses a church burial to the born-out-of-wedlock infant. And so Tess buries the boy herself in the countryside, which is now her habitat of choice.

Tess's prospects brighten when Angel Clare returns. She's working as a milkmaid and he's studying farming. Despite, or perhaps because of, his upper-middle-class upbringing, he's reading Karl Marx. But this aura of enlightenment proves thin. For after marrying Tess, he rejects her when she, honest as ever, tells the truth about herself and Alec. "I thought you were a child of nature but you're the last in a line of degenerate aristocrats," he says cruelly. And so she goes back to working in the fields and sleeping in the woods. She also goes back to Alec, who's happy to have a mistress and not a wife. Angel returns, contrite and determined to "save" her. But, as she sees it, the only way out is to dispatch with her tormentor.

Breaking with his usual depictions of violence, Polanski doesn't show the killing. Instead, we see a chambermaid discovering that the ceiling of the guesthouse foyer is dripping blood. Now Tess and Angel are on the run. They find a shuttered house and for a brief moment share some happiness. But the police finally catch up with them—at Stonehenge. As they're taken away, Tess quite calmly accepting her fate, it's clear Polanski is saying that the passions we've seen played out before us are as old as time itself.

Nastassja Kinski
in *Tess* (1979).

Following pages: Nastassja
Kinski in *Tess* (1979).

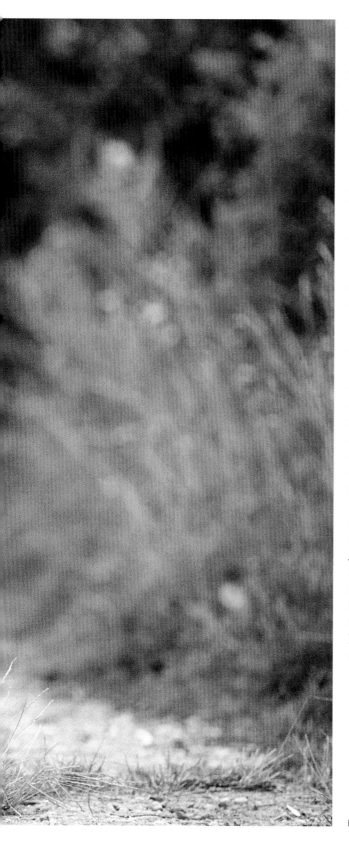

A movie for children

Oliver Twist (2005) is set in another time and was made for another reason. As Roman Polanski said when the movie was released: "I would never think of doing a movie for children if I did not have any. A lot of things in the film I know about. I relate to all the sufferings much more now that I have kids. I see it from the outside now. And before, I didn't. Children have this capacity for resistance, and they accept things as they are, maybe because they have no other reference. They are somehow more flexible; they adapt much faster than adults."[18]

Thus, Polanski's take is rather different than the two previous adaptations: David Lean's 1948 classic, with it's scene-devouring performance from Alec Guinness, and Carol Reed's 1968 Oscar-winning film version of Lionel Bart's musical *Oliver!*, with production numbers so lavish as to make the story's darkness seem almost out of character. For Polanski, as critic Roger Ebert noted, everything in Dickens was precisely *in character*: "Oliver is about 10 when he is taken into the world of Fagin and his young pickpockets, and Polanski was 10 in 1943, when his parents were removed by the Nazis from the Krakow ghetto and he was left on his own, moving from one temporary haven to another in the city and the countryside. In the black market economy of wartime Poland, he would have met or seen people like Fagin, Bill Sykes, Nancy and the Artful Dodger, resorting to thievery and prostitution to survive. In that sense, Oliver Twist more directly reflects his own experience than *The Pianist*."[19] An arguable point perhaps. But it's inarguable that Polanski was making the film for his children, both of whom have walk-ons in it (Elvis as a boy playing with a hoop on the streets of London, Morgane as a country farmer's daughter). Even more to the Polanskiesque point is Ben Kingsley's performance as Fagin.

Barney Clark in *Oliver Twist* (2005).

Fagin is not simply Jewish, he's been regarded in literary-historical terms as *The* Jew, right alongside Shylock in Shakespeare's *The Merchant of Venice*. Shylock, with his demand for "a pound of flesh" is almost entirely sinister; Fagin might be said to be merely "naughty." Dickens takes some care in creating this man who runs a pack of thieving street urchins so as not to evoke pedophilia too clearly. His incessant "my darlings" will do. Guinness in the Lean version leaves it at that, arousing criticism for his "Jewish" mannerisms (the "oily" voice, the furtive gestures, and facial expressions) coming close to outright caricature. Ron Moody in the Reed version is merely jolly and convivial. Ben Kingsley is something else. His Fagin isn't comic; he's a desperate man. And his relationship to the boys he manages is all business. One might say he's temperamentally "neutral," especially in contrast to the other adults who are depicted by Polanski with Dickensian relish for exposing human meanness and undisguised hatred of the poor.

Oliver's famous "Please Sir, I want some more" is greeted with an immediate smack—instead of an incredulous pause and no blow at all, as is usual. The world is mean, save for the boy's saviors—who rescue him at the last minute. But then there's Fagin who—Polanski makes certain to show, as in no previous film rendition—is going to face the gallows for his crimes.

"You were kind to me," says Oliver, visiting the sad old man in prison before his execution. It's not a line you'll find in Dickens. It comes straight from Polanski's heart.

Roman Polanski with Barney Clark
on the set of *Oliver Twist* (2005)

Opposite page: Ben Kingsley
in *Oliver Twist* (2005).

Polanskian politics
Death and the Maiden, The Pianist, The Ghost Writer

Ewan McGregor in
The Ghost Writer (2010).

It's what's underneath that counts

Polanski has never been what's usually thought of as a "political filmmaker." He traffics neither in agitprop (like Godard) nor protest drama (like Costa-Gavras). In fact one would be hard-pressed to say what his "politics" are in anything other than a very general, more or less "liberal" sense. Yet, while he hasn't formally chosen politics as a subject, he has been very much subject to politics personally throughout his life. First as a Jewish child on the run, then as a citizen of communist Poland, defying "Socialist Realism" with *Knife in the Water*, and more recently as a political pawn precariously placed at the tender mercies of the Los Angeles District Attorney's office, seeking his extradition on a statutory rape charge that had supposedly been settled years before.[20] As for anything approaching a verbal "statement," the closest Polanski has come was in 2008 when asked about his recollection of the 1968 Cannes Film Festival, which was abbreviated in response to the protests of workers and students that overtook France that year. Fellow filmmakers Godard and Truffaut were quite excited by May '68, but not Polanski. "I came from communist Poland, and I knew moments of elation like this where suddenly you just feel like you're doing something great, when in fact it's just an illusion."[21]

Still, his disinclination to believe in the "illusion" of protest politics doesn't mean Polanski has assumed a "passive" posture in his work. When the occasion presents itself, he has plenty to say. And not just in the implicit mode of *Chinatown*, with its epic exposure of municipal corruption, combined with murder and incest. His three most overtly political films, *Death and the Maiden* (1994), *The Pianist* (2002), and *The Ghost Writer* (2010), are quite explicit in their respective broadsides against state-sponsored terrorism and mass genocide, past and present. But as always with Polanski, whatever transpires on the surface, its what's underneath that counts the most.

"Be a good girl"

Adapted by Ariel Dorfman from his play of the same name, *Death and the Maiden* (1994) is set in an unnamed Latin American country that recently saw the overthrow of a murderous right-wing military junta. It also unfolds almost entirely in the highly circumscribed setting of a small house on a rocky oceanfront terrain on a dark and stormy night. In other words, it's as creepily cozy as *Knife in the Water*. 73

Polanski cuts from a concert featuring Schubert's String Quartet No. 14 in D Minor, from which the film gets its title (and which Polanski first used at the close of *What?*), to a shot of crashing waves and then to the film's heroine, Paulina Escobar (Sigourney Weaver). She is listening to a radio report about an ongoing investigation led by her husband Gerardo (Stuart Wilson) of political torture that took place years before. That her response to such news is to get herself a plate of food, go into a closet, sit on the floor, and eat is a preview of what's to follow. When she hears a car approaching she goes to get a gun. As it turns out, it's Gerardo, who has been given a lift as his car has broken down. "Be a good girl," she tells herself. But she can't because she recognizes the voice of the man who gave Gerardo the lift as Dr Roberto Miranda (Ben Kingsley), the man who had tortured her—something that Gerardo has yet to learn about. She hides in the bedroom, the better to listen them chatting blithely about "the female soul." As it's late, Miranda stays, sleeping on the living-room couch. Paulina sneaks out and pushes Miranda's

Above and opposite page: Ben Kingsley and Sigourney Weaver in *Death and the Maiden* (1994).

car over a cliff. When she returns to the house she wakens Miranda, pistol-whips him, ties him to a chair with duct tape, and stuffs a pair of her own panties in his mouth before taping it shut.

The casting of Weaver is crucial to this scene and everything that follows. Having fought off giant lethal interstellar creatures in *Alien*, she's more than up to the task of taking on Kingsley. Moreover, the determined resolve with which she strode through those sci-fi epics is most *apropos* in this intimate *mano-a-mano* context—though the stakes are higher because the psychological, far more than the physical, is involved.

Paulina informs her captive that he raped her fourteen times while a recording of Schubert's "Death and the Maiden" played. He denies it. The situation becomes further fraught as the ineffectual Gerardo—now awake and alarmed—gets a call from his superiors informing him that guards are being sent to the house because he has received death threats. From this point on the action becomes a cat-and-mouse game with cat and mouse changing places.

Miranda taunts Paulina, mentioning certain "wires" that were used for torture—even while denying he used them himself. He claims a call to Barcelona can clear him of any charge she wants to level and encourages Gerardo to make it. Gerardo is easily intimidated—which indicates why he was chosen for the investigation. But Paulina wants to take Miranda somewhere—to the edge of the cliff she's already pushed his car over—in order to kill him. It's there that he finally confesses to his crimes. But rather than express remorse, he tells her how much he enjoyed it. We've reached the point toward which this has all been heading. But rather than kill Miranda, Paulina unties him.

Suddenly we're back at the concert where the film began. Paulina and Gerardo are seated at the front. As the Schubert plays, Paulina glances up to see Miranda in a box with his family. Was it all a dream? To pose the question is like asking for a close-up of Rosemary's baby. What's important is the confrontation itself. And one can only wonder whether Polanski has ever harbored thoughts about facing off against his enemies in this fashion himself. 75

Nothing special about Szpilman

Indeed, eight years later, with *The Pianist*, Polanski does so, in a manner of speaking, through a dramatic surrogate. The subject this time is the Holocaust. And rather than seek the upbeat and heroic as Spielberg did with *Schindler's List* (1993), Polanski (with screenwriter Ronald Harwood) goes very downbeat with the decidedly un-heroic Wladyslaw Szpilman, a Jewish concert pianist who recounted in his memoir his escape from Nazi capture by hiding out in empty apartments in Warsaw, right under the Third Reich's nose. It's a tale of survival. But our survivor—played with enormous sad-eyed charm by Adrien Brody—is no noble character. He's just a man who made it through thanks to luck, and a couple of allies—while the rest of his family went straight to the camps and death. His musical talent may give him a touch of class, but there's nothing special about Szpilman—which is precisely why he's perfect for Polanski.

This is what characterizes our anti-hero. If he rises above the fray, not because he thinks he's in any way deserving. It's just that he's naturally optimistic. When his large, well-educated and fairly well-fixed family make plans to leave—only to discover that Britain and France, having declared war on Germany, are no longer safe havens—he doesn't register despair. When he and his girlfriend, a lovely gentile girl he's been wooing, discover they can no longer enter a favorite café because he's a Jew, he simply chats with her for awhile outside by its doorway—as if that were "date" enough.

Polanski next shows us the creation of the Warsaw ghetto where the city's Jews will be housed before being taken off to the extermination camps—a fate of which, at this point, they're unaware. Not that where they're living doesn't presage disaster. There are corpses lying in the streets, and fear runs rampant—underscored by a once-attractive old woman, with flaming red hair, who asks every passerby about the whereabouts of her husband. Worse still, we see German soldiers making fun of the elderly and the infirm as they wait at the gate to leave for jobs they still have elsewhere in the city. Kapos are recruited to keep the ghetto

Adrien Brody in
The Pianist (2002).

inmates "in line." But Szpilman doesn't join them, or the resistance either.

He passes the time playing piano in a ghetto café that tries to maintain an air of elegance in spite of everything. Men gamble. Women flirt with him. On the surface it seems almost normal. But Szpilman's far from being unaffected. For example, he tries to help a small boy trapped in a wall he's trying to crawl out of. The boy dies, but he's a representative of sorts for Polanski, who used to crawl back and forth through the walls of the Krakow ghetto. He, of course, lived, but others died, and this scene is about them.

Szpilman's father says American Jews should do more to oppose the Germans—a sentiment heard of in some American—Jewish quarters but not in others.[22]

While rumors of deportation to "work camps" circulate among the ghetto-dwellers, Szpilman gets a job in a clothing store, as do other members of his family. But it's scarcely a refuge, and finally everyone in the ghetto is herded into a large yard. The Szpilman family is pushed aboard the cattle cars headed for the death camps. But a kapo pulls Szpilman from the line, telling him, "Don't run." (This is from Polanski's very own memories.)

Below: Adrien Brody in
The Pianist (2002).

Opposite page: Adrien Brody and
Wanja Mues in *The Pianist* (2002).

In an enormously deep long shot we see Szpilman walking back through the ghetto. Nothing but wreckage and corpses. Underscoring this, Polanski cuts back to the yard from which the people had just been taken and put on trains. It's filled with the suitcases they were forced to leave behind. No need for belongings when you're on your way to die.

Later, as Spilzman is hiding in an abandoned flat—a familiar setting in Polanski's works—he witnesses from his window the Warsaw ghetto uprising, with people he once knew lined up and summarily shot. When things get quiet he goes scavenging for food. The city is an enormous expanse of ruins. He manages to find a large can of pickles—but no can opener. Lurching around the ruins, clinging to this can, he's a figure right out of the "Theater of the Absurd." As he tries to open the can with a pick he found in the street, he is discovered by a tall, smartly dressed German officer who asks Szpilman what he did before the war. When Szpilman tells him he was a pianist, the officer asks him to play the piano that happens to be in the room where they're standing. Szpilman, who hasn't played in years, sits down and swiftly launches into Chopin's Ballade no. 1 in G minor, opus 23. He then breaks down and cries.

His playing clearly cheered the officer, as he returns the next day with bread and jam. But Polanski doesn't treat this sequence as a means of demonstrating that man's humanity can blossom even in the most dire circumstances. When the Russian Army arrives, nearly killing him because they think he's a German, he learns of the officer's fate. He was taken away to a prison camp where he died, as we learn from the closing credits.

For the final sequence, in which we see Szpilman playing Chopin's Grande Polonaise Brillante for Piano and Orchestra, Polanski has taken care to avoid any sentimentalism. Thus, unlike *Schindler's List*, *The Pianist* leaves us with no sense of "uplift."

The Polanski affair

Brody won the Oscar for Best Actor for the title role and Polanski was duly awarded Best Director—but, unlike Brody, Polanski wasn't there to collect it. That's because of what happened on March 11, 1977, when Polanski was arrested in Los Angeles on charges of illegal sexual activity with a thirteen-year-old girl he was photographing for *Vogue* magazine. The girl, who in 2008 was formally identified as Samantha Geimer when she appeared in the documentary *Roman Polanski: Wanted and Desired*, has had little to say about the incident. Polanski was almost universally condemned. Only the noted novelist and historian Gore Vidal, in an interview published in *The Atlantic Monthly*, came to Polanski's vigorous defense:

> There was a totally different story at the time that doesn't resemble anything that we're now being told. The media can't get anything straight. Plus, there's usually an anti-Semitic and anti-fag thing going on with the press—lots of crazy things. The idea that this girl was in her communion dress, a little angel all in white, being raped by this awful Jew, Polacko—that's what people were calling him—well, the story is totally different now from what it was then.

And to put even a finer point on it, Vidal added, "Look, am I going to sit and weep every time a young hooker feels as though she's been taken advantage of?"[23]

In his memoir *Roman*, Polanski makes no excuses for himself, clearly embarrassed by the entire incident and lamenting its consequences. But the fact that he cannot return to the United States should in no way be regarded as a detriment to Polanski's career. Even had he never met Geimer, the studios that made *Rosemary's Baby* and *Chinatown*

possible wouldn't "green-light" them today. And the director of *Dance of the Vampires* clearly has film-making fantasy ideas well in advance of the likes of *Twilight* (2008).

However, while Polanski was through with Hollywood, the city of Los Angeles wasn't through with him, for on September 26, 2009, he was arrested in Switzerland on the request of the US authorities, jailed for two months, and put under house arrest in Gstaad while awaiting the results of his appeal to fight extradition to the US. Apparently, in the wake of the release of *Roman Polanski: Wanted and Desired* the filmmaker's legal counsel had made some inquiries as to how his legal status regarding the US might be resolved. This inspired the Los Angeles District Attorney (who was then running for Secretary of State) to arrange to nab Polanski. But the Swiss ultimately rejected the request, declaring the director a "free man" and therefore allowing him to put the finishing touches to *The Ghost Writer*, the film whose shooting had been completed just before his arrest, and whose editing had been executed during his incarceration via notes Polanski was able to pass to his editor, Hervé de Luze.

Cinematic felicities

Like *Rosemary's Baby*, this political thriller came into being almost by accident. Polanski had been planning a far more elaborate and expensive project with writer Robert Harris called *Pompeii*. Sending him a draft of its script, Harris included the proofs of *The Ghost*, the thriller he'd just finished writing. As *Pompeii* wasn't jelling and *The Ghost* excited him, Polanski proposed to Harris that they work on this instead. The result is arguably Polanski's most beautifully made, dramatically chilling, and politically astute film to date. The alleged difficulties Polanski might face by not being able to shoot in the US proved to be nonexistent. The beaches of the islands of Rømø (Denmark) and Sylt (Germany) worked perfectly well for Martha's Vineyard (the location for Spielberg's *Jaws* in 1975) in the bleak chill of winter. Plus CGI techniques made it possible to create a synthetic exterior outside the window of a studio set stand for the principle character's compound. Over and above all else, Polanski's phenomenally refined visual sense results in all sorts of cinematic felicities such as the opening shot, in which a ferry docking at Martha's Vineyard at night bears a striking resemblance to a phantom carriage in a film by F. W. Murnau. Cinematographer Pawel Edelman strikes a balance between the simplicity William A. Fraker brought to *Rosemary's Baby* and the lushness John A. Alonzo gave *Chinatown*. No wonder he's now Polanski's D.P. of choice.

The thing is, *The Ghost Writer* is not exactly a horror film, nor is it a standard thriller. Instead of locations evocative of sinister "Old World" atmosphere, it unfolds in a very bright and shiny modern world. What makes it malevolent is its calm. Moreover, it's largely uninhabited. At many points in the action, the film's anti-hero is completely alone. Yet so astute has Polanski been in constructing suspense that we're made aware that in locations seemingly copacetic he's a moving target for forces who would terminate him without thinking twice.

"Live with it"

Like the hitchhiker in *Knife in the Water* the protagonist of this thriller (played with light, offhand charm by Ewan McGregor) has no name. This perfectly suits his status as a ghostwriter chosen to anonymously liven up the otherwise leaden memoir of former

Seamless editing

While he first worked with Polanski in 1964 on 'La Rivière de Diamants', the Amsterdam episode of *The World's Most Beautiful Swindles*, Hervé de Luze doesn't appear amidst the director's filmography again until *Pirates* (1986). In the wake of that illstarred project, his Polanski association continues to this day. His predecessor, Alastair McIntyre, was the director's principle editor, starting with *Repulsion* (1965) and continuing on through to *Tess* (1979). What marks a classical filmmaker like Polanski is his insistence on "seamless" editing. He may specialize in suspense, horror, and the bizarre, but a thorough examination of his work reveals no cheap "shock cuts." Nothing is done "for effect." Everything that appears on screen is there to reveal character and advance the story. Consequently, where the image "falls" is of utmost importance.

One of the most beautiful examples of this can be found early in *The Ghost Writer* where we cut from a boat on a ferry carrying a mysteriously empty car to a beach upon which a body has washed up. It's a moment of maximum impact. Yet Polanski, who clearly shoots only what he needs for every situation, has done so with the understanding that de Luze has what might be called the musical eloquence to let each audio-visual integer shine. As a whole, *The Ghost Writer* is redolent with this sort of editorial sophistication. And it's all the more impressive when one knows that the director was first imprisoned and shortly afterward placed under house arrest while his film was being edited. That Polanski and de Luze found a way to communicate with one another during this incarceration speaks volumes of the editor's art—as well as the very great artist for whom he has served so splendidly.

Opposite page: Ewan McGregor in *The Ghost Writer* (2010).

The Ghost Writer (2010).

British Prime Minister Adam Lang (Pierce Brosnan), a politician who not only dragged his country into a US-sponsored foreign war, but "renditioned" foreign-born British citizens. We're told of several men he had had kidnapped in Pakistan and turned over for torture (aka "enhanced interrogation techniques") elsewhere. In other words, he's virtually Tony Blair. Because of the widespread public outrage his "renditioning" escapades have inspired, Lang has "jumped the pond" to the US, and is snugly ensconced in an ultramodern bunker-style dwelling provided for him by the large and decidedly sinister "Hatherton Group," a conglomerate clearly meant to invoke international oil behemoth Halliburton. In fact, Lang's situation is very much like that of former Halliburton chief and former US Vice President Dick Cheney, who (like his boss, George W. Bush) can no longer travel to certain foreign lands lest they risk being turned over to the World Court and put on trial for "Crimes Against Humanity."

The tale begins, however, not in the upper reaches of politics but on that ominous ferry docking in Martha's Vineyard. All the cars onboard

Above and opposite page:
Ewan McGregor in *The Ghost Writer* (2010).

The car scene

The Ghost Writer

"Auto-directional automobile devices" are nothing in and of themselves, but the scene in *The Ghost Writer* that features one is strikingly innovative for a mystery thriller. It's key to the mysterious death of Mike McCara—the ghostwriter originally hired by former British Prime Minister Adam Lang to write his memoir. The Ghost discovers a cache of McCara's photos in his room that indicate Lang isn't the "hail fellow well met" he's passed himself off as to the world, but a seasoned operative allied with dark "insider" forces.

He then takes another jaunt—this time in McCara's car. The pre-programmed mechanical voice of its "Connect-a-Drive" takes him to the home of ultra-insider professor Paul Emmett—clearly the mastermind behind Lang's political rise and the director of his actions *vis-à-vis* "extraordinary renditions" of suspected terrorists to foreign territories for the purposes of torture. Dramatically, a tense conversation between Emmett and The Ghost—in which the latter gently tries to cull information while the former remains as implacable as a mummy—is the highlight. But the real power of the sequence is found in the preceding one and is instilled by the insistent electronic voice: "In 50 yards, turn left." "After a mile, make a sharp right turn—turn left."

"In a few yards you will have reached your destination." It's a disembodied *memento mori*—Mike McCara speaking from beyond the grave and giving his successor clues about his death—which by this point we can clearly sense was murder.

drive off save one—which we quickly learn doesn't have a driver. It's an image right out of Fritz Lang's *The Thousand Eyes of Dr. Mabuse* (1960), and its sinister aura escalates when Polanski cuts from a tow trucker taking the car away, to a body that's just washed up on the nearby shore. It's the corpse of Mike McCara, an extremely close ally of Lang's who had been ghostwriting his memoir. As The Ghost quickly learns, no one in the Lang compound is even so much as slightly interested in solving the mystery of McCara's passing—though Amelia, Lang's PA, vouchsafes to The Ghost, "You could be the new Mike McCara." It's praise that also might be likened to a threat and a promise.

During the movie, personal issues are neatly dovetailed into "Matters of State" as The Ghost observes both the tension between Amelia and Lang's wife Ruth (who's quite aware that sexually she doesn't rate as high as her rival) and a scene where Lang is seen losing his cool, shouting furiously at someone on the phone. Increasingly harder to avoid is an enraged Englishman (David Rintoul) clearly modeled after American anti-Iraq War

activist Cindy Sheehan. He shows up not only in the bar of The Ghost's hotel (whispering "asshole" in his ear as he passes him by) but also leading a group of demonstrators outside the Hatherton-owned compound. And, unlike Sheehan, he's clearly dangerous.

Alone in the compound, in McCara's very room, The Ghost discovers a hidden cache of photos and documents revealing important information about Lang's past. For while claiming he entered politics quite casually, the better to impress his future wife Ruth, the fact is he was recruited by Ruth, who's far more than a "jealous wife."

The Ghost's inquiry continues until, taking the ferry back to Martha's Vineyard, he finds himself pursued by a pair of men obviously out to kill him—no doubt the same ones that had killed his predecessor. Leaving his car and jumping the fence back to the mainland, he checks in at the tiny hotel by the dock. A small block-like structure at the end of an empty parking lot, it's the most desolate image in all of Polanski's films—the ultimate cul-de-sac.

Later, Lang is shot by the British protester—dressed in a soldier's uniform—whereupon the latter

85

is shot and killed as well. The all-too-familiar tropes of the paranoid political thrillers of the 1970s (particularly The Parallax View) and its progeny (Warren Beatty's Bulworth) are now in place.

The movie ends with the death of The Ghost as a car looms up and—just out of frame—hits and kills him. Within the frame, the pages of the book, which have been found to be hiding a secret message, are scattered in the wind.

Yes, Jake, it's *Chinatown* once more. But we're not in LA, and the crimes that have been committed here are international. The guilty parties have not been prosecuted and never will be. This is a scenario that Polanski knows all too well from his own experience, and it's one we should recognize from ours. For the "Crimes Against Humanity" of the Bush administration, to which the film alludes, are well known to us—as is the fact that the subsequent Obama administration has no intention of prosecuting the offenders. This is why The Ghost's murder is executed by Polanski with such visual panache. It's just a flourish, really. And in the last moments of this—his most brilliantly conceived and executed (and, not unexpectedly, ignored in the US)—work, Polanski says to all of us, "*Live with it!*"

The problem is *we can*.

Above: Kim Cattrall, Olivia Williams, and Pierce Brosnan in *The Ghost Writer* (2010).

Opposite page: Ewan McGregor in *The Ghost Writer* (2010).

Following pages: *The Ghost Writer* (2010).

The perfect film

Carnage

Jodie Foster in
Carnage (2011).

Killing remarks

From the very outset of his career, Polanski has striven for maximum impact with an ecomomy of means. Yes, he's occasionally wandered into the warm waters of visual extravagance, but beneath the sensual *mise-en-scène* of *Dance of the Vampires* and *Chinatown* we find the same knife poised to strike as in *A Murderer*. What differentiates his most recent work, *Carnage* (2011), from the general run of the Polanski canon is it's explicitly lighthearted air. Menace and mayhem are still involved, but this time they're largely off screen, as Polanski zeroes in not on weapons but *words* that wound. *Carnage* is chockablock with "killing remarks," yet no one gets killed. For his subject is human folly at its most mundane—which is to say its most childish. By contrast, his methodology is scrupulously adult. His cast of four was given more than ample rehearsal time to calibrate every detail of character and "motivation." Then the fruits of their labors were ever so carefully inserted into a tightly constructed *mise-en-scène* in which a traditionally circumscribed Polanski setting appears quite spacious and free, even as the characters within it act as if its walls were closing in tighter and tighter with every passing moment.

Polanski's cinematic delivery device is *God of Carnage*, a play by Yasmina Reza successfully performed in France and, in English translation, in Great Britain and America.[24] A beautifully constructed play, it deals with two couples who meet to discuss an altercation that has taken place between their respective children. On stage this fight isn't seen at all. But in Polanski's adaptation (which he co-scripted with Reza) we get a brief but telling soupçon—a long shot of a playground where a small group of boys are talking (their words inaudible to us) with some degree of excitement, climaxed by one of them (played by Elvis Polanski) hauling off and hitting another boy with a stick. The other boys gather round the injured party. Its effect is along the lines of Hitchcock's *Rope* (1948), in which the opening shot reveals the strangling of a young man, the rest of the film exploring the consequences of this act. And like *Rope*, *Carnage* sticks to a single set (until its very last shot, which returns to the playground).

With *Rope*, Hitchcock was attempting a technical *tour de force* in which a series of ten-minute takes could be strung together to create the impression that the entire film was made in one shot—a "perfect film" to match the "perfect crime" its villainous heroes have committed. But neither the crime

Christoph Waltz and Kate Winslet in *Carnage* (2011).

nor the *mise-en-scène* is quite perfect. The color cameras of that era could execute takes of a maximum of only ten minutes. Hitchcock was thus forced to dolly in to the back of an actor's jacket, and in one instance resorted to a standard piece of cross-cutting as one ten-minute reel came to an end and a new one began. Polanski cuts freely and frequently, multiplying shots of the set created by Dean Tavoularis—the nicely, but not ostentatiously, decorated Manhattan apartment of Michael and Penelope Longstreet (John C. Reilly and Jodie Foster), a couple who we quickly learn have an exceedingly high opinion of themselves. So crime is not the issue here, but rather everyday social interaction—which, in crisis, as Polanski shows, may become criminal after all.

God of Carnage

The Longstreet boy was the one struck with a stick. And as the action proper begins we're introduced to the parents of his attacker, Alan and Nancy Cowan (Christoph Waltz and Kate Winslet) who have been invited over to "settle things," as it were. The smile of triumph on Penelope's face as she finishes typing the "statement" that the couples have agreed to co-sign is pivotal to Polanski, who spends the rest of the film wiping off that smile.

Between dessert and liqueurs, we observe an escalation in the unfolding of the action and in the change of tone used by the characters. Penelope is anxious that the boys have a meeting so that the Cowan child can apologize to their son. She's quite concerned that he should be aware of what he's done, and is more than a little put out when Nancy vouchsafes that he "hasn't really talked about it." Alan is far more blunt: "My son is a maniac." This doesn't disturb him at all, however, as he says he believes in the "God of Carnage." Life to him is nothing but chaotic violence. And one doesn't have to be the proverbial rocket scientist to guess that Polanski concurs with this sentiment to some degree, although he wouldn't express the belief so glibly.

Violence of a far more "civilized" sort soon transpires over dessert. There's a wonderful look of resentment on Penelope's face when she and Michael are in the kitchen preparing to dish out plates of this supposed treat to their guests. It's just a fleeting expression but it's telling enough to indicate that she's feigning "graciousness" towards people she truly despises. What she wants is social approval. Consequently she's at pains to emphasize how unique this dessert supposedly is, composed as it is of both apples and pears (each fruit having to be sliced at different widths) with the whole encased in gingerbread crumbs. In short, the Longstreets are pretentious "yuppies," to the manner born. Penelope's insistence that the Cowans be impressed by the dessert is identical to her insistence that the boys get together so that the perpetrator can "apologize" to his victim. Clearly this isn't going to happen. But what makes this bad situation hilariously worse is when Nancy—to whom

Penelope has ill-advisedly given some warm Coke to "settle" what's originally claimed to be a slightly upset stomach—suddenly projectile-vomits the dessert she's just eaten all over the Longstreets' art-book-filled coffee table.

"My Kokoschka!" Penelope screams—as if Nancy's upchuck were every bit as egregious as her son's stick-wielding. Penelope, who's anxious to let everyone know she's writing a book about "the Darfur tragedy," even while feigning modesty by claiming she's not "really" a writer, is exceptionally put out by the way everything has been proceeding—which is to say not by the rules she's established for everyone else to live by. And those rules apparently don't include Michael being so generous with the expensive aged Scotch he offers to an eager Alan.

And then there's the hamster. "You got rid of the hamster?," a shocked Nancy asks Michael early on in the proceedings when he casually tells her his daughter's pet so disgusted him that he let it out of its cage onto the street, telling the child that it "ran away." This passive violence upsets the woman far more than the active violence perpetrated by her

Jodie Foster and John C. Reilly in *Carnage* (2011).

son. But it's indicative of the tapestry of myopic self-interest that Polanski has been underscoring, along with the running gag of the Cowans attempting to leave the Longstreet's apartment over and over again, only to be stopped by a phone call from Walter and dragged back by an offer of one form of food or drink or another. Think of a cross between *Who's Afraid of Virginia Woolf?* and *The Exterminating Angel*, plus a soupçon of *Seinfeld*, and you've got it.

As the film is not over, Polanski cuts from this postmodern update of Jean-Paul Sartre's discovery that "Hell is other people," to a close-up of ... the hamster. He's outside in the park, apparently safe and freely gamboling about. In short, we have the one unreservedly happy ending in the entire oeuvre of Polanski. And, to top it off, we see the boys whose fight provoked the entire parental uproar chatting amiably with one another.

Have we turned a corner? Is the malevolent Polanski of old no more. Has he "mellowed with age," choosing the "filmed theater" mode of Sacha Guitry (*Faisons un Rêve*, 1936) and Alain Resnais (*Mélo*, 1986) as his ideal cinematic form?

Perhaps not. For Polanski has announced that his next project, entitled *D* will concern the Dreyfus affair, the tumultuous scandal of the late 1890's in which Alfred Dreyfus a young French artillery officer of Jewish descent was sentenced to life imprisonment for the false accusation communicating French military secrets. Novelist Emile Zola came to Dreyfus' defense, the case was reopened and Dreyfus was pardoned. But not before the entire affair upended French society Polanski who is writing the script with his collaborator on *The Ghost Writer*, Robert Harris says. "I have long wanted to make a film about the Dreyfus Affair, treating it not as a costume drama but as a spy story. In this way one can show its absolute relevance to what is happening in today's world— — the age-old spectacle of the witch-hunt of a minority group, security paranoia, secret military tribunals, out-of-control intelligence agencies, governmental cover-ups and a rabid press."

And no one is better to this than Roman Polanski.

John C. Reilly, Jodie Foster, Christoph Waltz et Kate Winslet in *Carnage* (2011).

Chronology

1933
18 August. Rajmund Roman Liebling born in Paris, France, to Bula (née Katz-Przedborska) and Ryszard Liebling (aka Ryszard Polanski), a painter and plastics manufacturer.

1936
Family returns to Poland.

1939–43
The Germans invade Poland and the family is sent to the Krakow ghetto. His mother is taken to Auschwitz and exterminated on arrival. Polanski witnesses his father's capture and, at age seven, escapes the ghetto, wandering through the Polish countryside pretending to be a Roman Catholic visiting his relatives.

1945
Reunited with his father who sends him to technical school. He takes up acting, becoming a child star on the radio.

1950–5
Studies at the Lodz National Film School. Appears in Andrzej Wajda's *A Generation*. Makes his first short film, *Rower* (1955).

1956–61
His short films *Two Men and A Wardrobe* (1958), *The Fat and the Lean* (1961), and *Mammals* (1962) begin to win him attention. Marries actress Barbara Lass in 1959. They divorce in 1961.

1962
Knife in the Water, his first feature, debuts and becomes an international sensation.

1964–6
In England, makes *Repulsion* (1965), an international hit, followed by *Cul-de-sac* (1966). Both are co-scripted by Gérard Brach.

1967
Makes *Dance of the Vampires* and falls in love with its female lead, Sharon Tate.

1968
January 20. Marries Sharon Tate. *Rosemary's Baby*, his first American film, is a smash hit.

1969
Sharon Tate, eight months pregnant with what would have been his first child, is murdered, along with several of their friends, by the Charles Manson "family," at the home belonging to musician Terry Melcher on Cielo Drive, Benedict Canyon, Los Angeles. Polanski is in Europe at the time.

1971
In England, makes film adaptation of Shakespeare's *Macbeth*, his first film since the tragedy.

1972
Now based in Europe, directs *What?* in Italy.

1973–4
Drawn back to America by producer Robert Evans to make *Chinatown*.

1977
Arrested for alleged rape of Samantha Geimer, a thirteen-year-old girl he was photographing for Paris *Vogue*. Pleads guilty to one count of unlawful sexual intercourse with a minor. Incarcerated for "psychiatric evaluation" in Chino State Prison.

1978
1 February. Is told by his attorney that despite the fact that the prosecuting attorneys recommend probation, "the judge could no longer be trusted …" and the judge's representations are "worthless." Polanski flees to France hours before sentencing by the judge.

Roman Polanski around 1946.

Two Men and a Wardrobe (1958).

Roman Polanski with Catherine Deneuve on the set of *Repulsion* (1965).

Zygmunt Malanowicz and Leon Niemczyk in *Knife in the Water* (1962).

Cul-de-sac (1966).

Roman Polanski and Sharon Tate in *Dances of the Vampires* (1967).

Roman Polanski on the set of *Pirates* (1986).

1981

Directs and stars in a production of Peter Shaffer's *Amadeus* first staged in Warsaw and then in Paris.

1988

Samantha Geimer sues Polanski, alleging "sexual assault, intentional infliction of emotional distress," and "seduction." Polanski agrees to a monetary settlement. Stars in Steven Berkoff's stage adaptation of Franz Kafka's *Metamorphosis* in Paris.

1989

30 August. Marries Emmanuelle Seigner.

1991

President of the jury of the Cannes Film Festival.

1993

20 January. Daughter Morgane is born.

1994

Co-stars with Gérard Depardieu in Giuseppe Tornatore's *A Pure Formality*.

1996

Directs Fanny Ardant in Paris production of Terence McNally's *Master Class*.

1997

In Vienna, directs *Tanz der Vampire*, a musical comedy based in part on his film classic.

1998

12 April. Son Elvis is born. Becomes a member of the Académie des Beaux-Arts of the Institut de France, succeeding the late Marcel Carné.

1999

Directs the stage production of Peter Schaffer's *Amadeus* in Milan.

2002

Stars in Andrzej Wajda's *Zemsta* (*The Revenge*). Receives the Golden Scepter, awarded by the Foundation of Polish Culture.

2003

Receives Academy Award for Best Director for *The Pianist*, which is collected by actor Harrison Ford on his behalf.

2009

26 September. Arrested in Switzerland at the request of the US authorities. Imprisoned in a jail near Zurich for two months, then put under house arrest at his home in Gstaad, awaiting appeal decision regarding US extradition demand. While in jail, Polanski edits his film *The Ghost Writer*.

2010

12 July . Swiss authorities release Polanski from custody, rejecting US extradition. All six of the original charges still remain pending in the US.

2011

10 March. During a television interview, Samantha Geimer accuses reporters, the media, and the judicial process of causing "way more damage to [her] and her family than anything Roman Polanski has ever done"—a statement markedly different from any she had given before, even in the documentary *Roman Polanski: Wanted and Desired*. Polanski makes a cameo appearance in his film *Carnage*.

Roman Polanski on the set of *Pirates* (1986).

Roman Polanski on the set of *Frantic* (1988).

Roman Polanski on the set of *Frantic* (1988).

Roman Polanski with Johnny Depp on the set of *The Ninth Gate* (1999).

Roman Polanski with Kim Katrall on the set of *The Ghost Writer* (2010).

Roman Polanski on the set of *The Ghost Writer* (2010).

Filmography

ACTOR ONLY

Trzy opowiesci   1953
'Jacek' segment
by Konrad Nalecki
Godzina bez slonca   1955
by Pawel Komorowski
A Generation   1955
by Andrzej Wajda
Zaczarowany rower   1955
by Silik Sternfeld
Nikodem Dyzma   1956
by Jan Rybkowski
Wraki   1957
by Ewa Petelska and Czeslaw Petelski
Koniec nocy   1957
by Julian Dziedzina, Pawel Komorowski and Walentyna Maruszewska
**What Will My Wife
Say To This?**   1958
by Jaroslav Mach
Speed   1959
by Andrzej Wajda
Bad Luck   1960
by Andrzej Munk
Do widzenia, do jutra   1960
by Janusz Morgenstern
Niewinni czarodzieje   1960
by Andrzej Wajda
Ostroznie, Yeti!   1961
by Andrzej Czekalski
Samson   1961
by Andrzej Wajda
The Magic Christian   1969
by Joseph McGrath
**Blood for Dracula
(aka Andy Warhol's
Dracula)**   1974
by Paul Morrissey
Chassé-croisé   1982
by Arielle Dombasle
En attendant Godot   1989
A television production of Samuel Beckett's play
by Walter D. Asmus
Back in the USSR   1992
by Deran Sarafian
A Pure Formality   1994
by Giuseppe Tornatore
**Tribute to Alfred
Lepetit**   2000
by Jean Rousselot
**Roman Polanski
Scene by Scene**   2000
by Mark Cousins
The Revenge   2002
by Andrzej Wajda
Rush Hour 3   2007
by Brett Ratner
Quiet Chaos   2008
by Antonello Grimaldi

SHORT FILMS

Rower   1955
Format 35 mm. **Produced by** Lodz school. **Running time** unknown (movie lost). With Adam Fiut, Roman Polanski.
• A boy wants to buy a bike.
A Murderer
Format 35 mm. **Produced by** Lodz School. **Running time** 1 min. 27. With school students.
• A man enters a room and stabs a sleeping man.
Teeth/Smile   1957
Format 35 mm. **Produced by** Lodz School. **Running time** 2 mins. With Kola Todorov.
• A voyeur is watching a naked woman in a bathtub through a window.
**Break Up The Dance/
We Destroy This Party** 1957
Format 35 mm. **Produced by** Lodz School. **Running time** 8 mins. With school students.
• Students crash a party given by other students.
**Two Men
and A Wardrobe**   1958
Format 35 mm. **Music** by Krzysztof Komeda. **Produced by** Lodz School. **Running time** 15 mins. With Jakub Goldberg, Henryk Kluba, Andrzej Kondratiuk, Barbara Lass, Stanislaw Michalski, Roman Polanski.
• Two men emerge from the ocean with a wardrobe that they carry around a town before returning to the ocean.
The Lamp   1959
Format 35 mm. **Produced by** Lodz School. **Running time** 7 mins 20. With Roman Polanski.
• The life of a toy shop at night.
When An Angel Falls 1959
Format 35 mm. **Produced by** Lodz School. **Running time** 21 mins. With Barbara Lass, Roman Polanski, Henryk Kluba, Andrzej Kondratiuk.
• An old woman working in a public lavatory is visited by the spirit of her dead son.
The Fat and the Lean 1961
Format 35 mm. **Music** by Krzysztof Komeda. **Produced by** Claude Jourdioux/APEC. **Running time** 15 mins. With André Katelbach, Roman Polanski.
• A master (fat) and his slave (lean) go through their daily routine.
Mammals   1962
Format 35 mm. **Produced by** Films Polski/Studio Se-ma-for. **Running time** 10 mins 30. With Henryk Kluba, Michal Zolnierkiewicz, Wojtek Frykowski.
• A "master" and "slave" pair change roles while cavorting on a ski slope. An outsider intervenes.
**'La Rivière de Diamants'/
'Amsterdam' episode
of The World's Most
Beautiful Swindles**   1964
Format 35 mm. **Produced by** Pierre Roustang. **Running time** 10 mins. With Nicole Karen, Jan Teulings, Arnold Gelderman.
• A beautiful young woman pulls off a diamond heist in broad daylight.
**'Cinéma Erotique'
episode of To Each
His Own Cinema**   2007
Running time 2 mins. 48. With Jean-Claude Dreyfus, Edith le Merdy, Michel Vuillermoz, Denis Podalydès, Sara Forestier.
• A couple in a theater watching a film are disturbed by the moaning noises made by another moviegoer.

FEATURE FILMS

Knife in the Water   1962
B&W. **Screenplay** Jakub Goldberg, Roman Polanski, Jerzy Skolimowski. **Cinematography** Jerzy Lipman. **Production design** Boleslaw Kamykowski. **Editing** Halina Prugar-Ketling. **Music** Krzysztof Komeda **Producer** Stanislaw Zylewicz **Running time** 1h 34. With Leon Niemczyk (Andrzej), Jolanta Umecka (Krystyna), Zygmunt Malanowicz (Hitchhiker), Anna Ciepielewska (Krystyna voiceover), Roman Polanski (Hitchhiker voiceover).
• A married couple takes a hitchhiker with them on a weekend boating trip, with unsettling results.

Repulsion   1965
B&W. **Screenplay** Roman Polanski, Gérard Brach, David Stone. **Cinematography** Gilbert Taylor. **Editing** Alastair McIntyre. **Music** Chico Hamilton. **Producer** Gene Gutowski. **Running time** 1h 45. With Catherine Deneuve (Carole), Ian Hendry (Michael), John Fraser (Colin), Yvonne Furneaux (Helen).
• A young beautician, haunted by paranoid visions of sexual attack, becomes a psychotic killer.

Cul-de-Sac   1966
B&W **Screenplay** Roman Polanski, Gérard Brach. **Cinematography** Gilbert Taylor. **Production design** Voytek. **Editing** Alastair McIntyre. **Music** Krzysztof Komeda. **Producers** Gene Gutowski, Michael Klinger, Tony Tenser. **Running time** 1h 53. With Donald Pleasence (George), Françoise Dorléac (Teresa), Lionel Stander (Dickie), Jack MacGowran (Albie), Ian Quarrier (Christopher). A married couple on a Northumberland island find their lives disrupted when a pair of gangsters on the run invade their home.

Dance of the Vampires
(The Fearless Vampire Killers)   ·1967
Screenplay Gérard Brach, Roman Polanski. **Cinematography** Douglas Slocombe. **Production design** Wilfred Shingleton. **Editing** Alastair McIntyre. **Music** Krzysztof Komeda. **Producers** Gene Gutowski, Martin Ransohoff. **Running time** 1h 48. With Jack MacGowran (Professor Abronsius), Roman Polanski (Alfred), Ferdy Mayne (Count von Krolock), Sharon Tate (Sarah Shagal), Alfie Bass (Shagal, the Innkeeper), Iain Quarrier (Herbert von Krolock).
• Traveling through Transylvania, self-styled vampire expert and his assistant meet a vampire Count and his family who have abducted a beautiful young girl for their annual ball.

Rosemary's Baby   1968
Screenplay Roman Polanski, based on the novel by Ira Levin. **Cinematography** William A. Fraker. **Production design** Richard Sylbert **Editing** Sam O'Steen, Bob Wyman. **Music** Krzysztof Komeda (as Christopher Komeda). **Producer** William Castle. **Running time** 1h 76. With Mia Farrow (Rosemary Woodhouse), John Cassavetes (Guy Woodhouse), Ruth Gordon (Minnie Castevet), Sidney Blackmer (Roman Castevet), Maurice Evans (Hutch), Ralph Bellamy (Dr. Sapirstein).
• The wife of an ambitious young actor comes to believe he's promised their firstborn child to a coven of witches who live in their apartment building in New York City.

Macbeth   1971
Screenplay Roman Polanski, Kenneth Tynan, adapted from play by William Shakespeare. **Cinematography** Gilbert Taylor. **Production design** Wilfred Shingleton. **Editing** Alastair McIntyre. **Music** Third Ear Band. **Producers** Andrew Braunsberg, Timothy Burrill, Hugh Hefner. **Running time** 2h 20. With Jon Finch (Macbeth), Francesca Annis (Lady Macbeth), Martin Shaw (Banquo), Terence Bayler (Macduff).
• Shakespeare's tragedy of a Scottish warrior who, tempted by the prophecy of a coven of witches, slaughters a monarch to gain his throne.

What?   1972
Screenplay Roman Polanski, Gérard Brach. **Cinematography** Marcello Gatti, Giuseppe Ruzzolini. **Production design** Aurelio Crugnola. **Editing** Alastair McIntyre. **Music** Claudio Gizzi. **Producer** Carlo Ponti. **Running time** 1h 54. With Sydne Rome (Nancy), Marcello Mastroianni (Alex), Hugh Griffith (Mr. Noblart), Romolo Valli (Giovanni), Roman Polanski (Mosquito, uncredited).
• A nubile half-naked innocent, hitchhiking through Europe, takes refuge in an Italian villa and encounters all manner of strange people and situations.

Chinatown   1974
Screenplay Robert Towne. **Cinematography** John A. Alonzo. **Production design** Richard Sylbert. **Editing** Sam O'Steen. **Music** Jerry Goldsmith. **Producer** Robert Evans. **Running time** 2h 10. With Jack Nicholson (J. J. Gittes), Faye Dunaway (Evelyn Mulwray), John Huston (Noah Cross), Roman Polanski (Man with Knife).
• In 1940s Los Angeles, a small-time private eye becomes involved in a complex case involving money, murder, and the city's land and water rights.

The Tenant   1976
Screenplay Roman Polanski, Gérard Brach, based on the novel by Roland Topor. **Cinematography** Sven Nykvist. **Production design** Pierre Guffroy. **Editing** Françoise Bonnot. **Music** Philippe Sarde. **Producers** Andrew Braunsberg, Alain Sarde. **Running time** 2h 06. With Roman Polanski (Trelkovsky), Isabelle Adjani (Stella), Melvyn Douglas (Monsieur Zy), Jo Van Fleet (Madame Dioz), Shelley Winters (The Concierge), Lila Kedrova (Madame Gaderian).
• A clerk rents an apartment whose previous tenant committed suicide, and becomes convinced other tenants want him to suffer the same fate.

Tess   1979
Screenplay Gérard Brach, Roman Polanski, John Brownjohn, based on the novel *Tess of the d'Ubervilles* by Thomas Hardy. **Cinematography** Ghislain Cloquet, Geoffrey Unsworth. **Production design** Pierre Guffroy. **Editing** Alastair McIntyre, Tony Priestley. **Music** Philippe Sarde. **Producer** Claude Berri. **Running time** 3h 06. With Nastassja Kinski (Tess), Leigh Lawson (Alec d'Uberville), Peter Firth (Angel Clare).
• The distant relative of a wealthy family, a young needy girl requests their help. Mistreated by a seducer and then by an idealist, Tess attempts to remain true to her moral values.

Pirates   1986
Screenplay John Brownjohn, Roman Polanski, Gérard Brach. **Cinematography** Witold Sobocinski. **Production design** Pierre Guffroy. **Editing** Hervé de Luze, William Reynolds. **Music** Philippe Sarde. **Producer** Tarak Ben Ammar. **Running time** 2h 01. With Walter Matthau (Captain Red), Cris Campion (The Frog), Damien Thomas (Don Alfonso de la Torré), Charlotte Lewis (María-Dolores de la Jenya de la Calde).
• A pirate captain and his faithful assistant take over a ship and head off in search of gold and adventure.

Frantic   1988
Screenplay Roman Polanski, Gérard Brach. **Cinematography** Witold Sobocinski. **Production** design Pierre Guffroy. **Editing** Sam O'Steen. **Music** Ennio Morricone. **Producers** Thom Mount, Tim Hampton. **Running time** 2h 00. With Harrison Ford (Dr. Richard Walker), Emmanuelle Seigner (Michelle), Betty Buckley (Sondra Walker), Roman Polanski (Taxi Driver).
• When an American doctor visiting Paris discovers that his wife has mysteriously vanished, a girl from the city's underworld comes to his aid.

Bitter Moon   1992
Screenplay Gérard Brach, John Brownjohn, based on the novel *Bitter Moon* by Pascal Bruckner. **Cinematography** Tonino Delli Colli. **Production design** Willy Holt, Gérard Viard. **Editing** Hervé de Luze. **Music** Vangelis. **Producers** Roman Polanski, Alain Sarde. **Running time** 2h 19. With Peter Coyote (Oscar), Emmanuelle Seigner (Mimi), Hugh Grant (Nigel), Kristin Scott Thomas (Fiona).
• On an ocean voyage, a young British couple meets a wheelchair-bound cynic and his sexually rapacious wife, whose tumultuous relationship is disclosed in a series of flashbacks.

Death and the Maiden   1994
Screenplay Rafael Yglesias and Ariel Dorfman, based on the latter's play. **Cinematography** Tonino Delli Colli. **Production design** Pierre Guffroy. **Editing** Hervé de Luze. **Music** Wojciech Kilar. **Producers** Thom Mount, Josh Kramer. **Running time** 1h 43. With Sigourney Weaver (Paulina Escobar), Ben Kingsley (Dr. Roberto Miranda), Stuart Wilson (Gerardo Escobar), Krystia Mova (Dr. Miranda's wife).
• A survivor of political torture captures the man who tortured her and tries to goad him into confessing his crimes.

The Ninth Gate   1999
Screenplay John Brownjohn, Enrique Urbizu, Roman Polanski,   99

based on the novel **The Club** Dumas by Arturo Pérez-Reverte. **Cinematography** Darius Khondji. **Production design** Dean Tavoularis. **Editing** Hervé de Luze. **Music** Wojciech Kilar. **Producer** Roman Polanski. **Running time** 2h 13. With Johnny Depp (Dean Corso), Frank Langella (Boris Balkan), Lena Olin (Lian Telfer), Emmanuelle Seigner (The Girl).
• A rare book scout is hired by a mysterious millionaire to find the three remaining copies of an occult manuscript that will grant him Satanic power.

The Pianist   2002
Screenplay Ronald Harwood, based on the memoir by Wladyslaw Szpilman. **Cinematography** Pawel Edelman. **Production design** Allan Starski. **Editing** Hervé de Luze. **Music** Wojciech Kilar. **Producers** Robert Benmussa, Roman Polanski. **Running time** 2h 30. With Adrien Brody (Wladyslaw Szpilman), Emilia Fox (Dorota), Frank Finlay (Father), Thomas Kretschmann (Captain Wilm Hosenfeld).
• A concert pianist escapes the Warsaw ghetto, and the death camps to which his family has been taken, hiding out in abandoned apartments throughout the long course of the war.

Oliver Twist   2005
Screenplay Ronald Harwood, based on the novel by Charles Dickens. **Cinematography** Pawel Edelman **Production design** Allan Starski. **Editing** Hervé de Luze. **Music** Rachel Portman. **Producers** Roman Polanski, Alain Sarde. **Running time** 2h 10. With Barney Clark (Oliver), Ben Kingsley (Fagin), Jeremy Swift (Mr. Bumble).
• Charles Dickens' tale of an orphan who finds a family among a gang of thieves.

The Ghost Writer   2010
Screenplay Robert Harris and Roman Polanski, based on the former's novel, *The Ghost*. **Cinematography** Pawel Edelman. **Production design** Albrecht Konrad. **Editing** Hervé de Luze. **Music** Alexandre Desplat. **Producers** Robert Benmussa, Alain Sarde, Roman Polanski. **Running time** 2h 08. With Ewan McGregor (The Ghost), Pierce Brosnan (Adam Lang), Olivia Williams (Ruth Lang), Kim Cattrall (Amelia Bly), Tom Wilkinson (Paul Emmett).
• A professional ghostwriter is hired to work on the memoir of a controversial British Prime Minister when the man previously assigned to the job dies mysteriously.

Carnage   2011
Screenplay Yasmina Reza and Roman Polanski, based on the former's play, *God of Carnage*. **Cinematography** Pawel Edelman. **Production design** Dean Tavoularis. **Editing** Hervé de Luze. **Music** Alexandre Desplat. **Producer** Saïd Ben Saïd. **Running time** 1h 20. With Jodie Foster (Penelope Longstreet), Kate Winslet (Nancy Cowan), Christoph Waltz (Alan Cowan), John C. Reilly (Michael Longstreet), Roman Polanski (Man behind the door, uncredited).
• Two married couples whose respective sons have been involved in a playground altercation meet to resolve the situation amicably. But good intentions quickly degenerate.

SCREENPLAYS DIRECTED BY OTHERS

A Taste for Women   1964
Co-written with Gérard Brach, Georges Bardawil, and Jean Léon. Directed by Jean Léon.

Love Story: "The Girl Opposite"   1965
Episode of TV series. Directed by Lionel Harris.

The Girl Across the Way   1968
Co-written with Gérard Brach. Directed by Jean-Daniel Simon.

The Boat on the Grass   1971
Co-written with Gérard Brach. Directed by Gérard Brach.

A Day at the Beach   1972
Co-written with Heere Heeresma. Directed by Simon Hesera.

Selected bibliography

Paul Cronin (ed.), *Roman Polanski: Interviews*, University of Mississippi Press, Jackson, 2005.

Ewa Mazierska, *Roman Polanski: The Cinema of a Cultural Traveller*, I. B. Tauris, London, 2007.

John Orr and Elzbieta Ostrowska (eds), *The Cinema of Roman Polanski: Dark Spaces of the World*, Wallflower Press, London, 2006.

Roman Polanski, *Roman by Polanski*, William Morrow and Company, New York, 1984.

Opposite page: Ewan McGregor on the set of *The Ghost Writer* (2010).

Notes

1. Roman Polanski, *Roman by Polanski*, William Morrow and Company, New York, 1984.

2. Raymond Durgnat, *Sexual Alienation in the Cinema: The Dynamics of Sexual Freedom*, Studio Vista, London, 1972, pp. 193–5.

3. Michel Delahaye and Jean-Andre Fieschi, "Landscape of a Mind: Interview with Roman Polanski," *Cahiers du cinéma*, 175 (February 1966).

4. Constantine Nasr, "Dancing with the Master: Roman Polanski remembers the making of *The Vampire Killers*," *Little Shoppe of Horrors*, 27 (2011).

5. Michel Delahaye and Jean-Andre Fieschi, op. cit.

6. Lillian Ross, *Picture*, Rinehart, New York, 1952; Anchor Books, New York, 1993, with foreword by Anjelica Huston.

7. Andrew Sarris, "Rosemary's Baby," *The Village Voice*, XIII, 41 (July 25, 1968); reprinted in Andrew Sarris, *Confessions of a Cultist: On the Cinema 1955–1969*, Simon and Schuster, New York, 1970, p. 373.

8. Will Elder and Harvey Kurtzman, *Little Annie Fanny, Volume 1: 1962–1970* and *Little Anne Fanny, Volume 2: 1970–1988*, Dark Horse Press, Milwaukie, OR, 2001.

9. Roland Topor, *The Tenant (Le Locataire chimérique)*, Phébus, Paris, 1964.

10. Carey McWilliams, *Southern California Country: An Island on the Land (1946)*, Gibbs Smith, Utah, 1980.

11. Robert Evans, *The Kid Stays in the Picture*, Hyperion, New York, 1994.

12. Raymond Chandler, *Trouble is My Business (1950)*, Vintage Books, New York, 1988.

13. *Roman by Polanski*, op. cit.

14. Jessica Winter, "Death Valley '74: The Desert of the Steal," *The Village Voice*, August 5, 2003.

15. *Roman by Polanski*, op. cit.

16. Jessica Winter, op. cit.

17. Janet Maslin, *Tess* (review), *New York Times*, December 12, 1980.

18. John Horn, "Polanski's Children", *Los Angeles Times*, September 18, 2005.

19. Roger Ebert, *Oliver Twist* (review), *Chicago Sun-Times*, September 30, 2005.

20. Kate Connolly, "Roman Polanski escapes extradition to US," *The Guardian*, July 12, 2010.

21. Tobias Grey, "Flashback: Cannes 1968—Polanski, Forman discuss year fest was stopped", *Variety*, May 8, 2008.

22. See David Ehrenstein, *Film: The Front Line—1984*, Arden Press, 1984: chapter about Laurence Jarvik's documentary *Who Shall Live and Who Shall Die* (1982).

23. John Meroney, "A Conversation with Gore Vidal," *The Atlantic Monthly*, October 2009.

24. Yasmina Reza, *The God of Carnage*, London, Faber and Faber, 2008.

Sources

British Film Institute: pp. 63, 66–7.
Collection Cahiers du cinéma: inside front cover, pp. 8, 9, 10, 34–5, 44–5, 46, 47, 48, 58–9, 68–9, 72, 74, 82, 83, 84, 86, 87, 88–9, 96 (1st col. bottom; 2nd col. bottom; 3rd col.; 4th col.), 97 (1st col.; 4th col.), 99 (3rd col. middle), 101.

Collection CAT'S: pp. 2–3, 20, 22–3, 24, 26–7, 29, 30, 40–1, 42, 50, 52–3, 54–5, 56, 62, 65, 76–7, 78, 79, 80, 90, 92, 93, 94–5.
Collection Christophel: cover, pp. 18, 32–3, 36, inside back cover.
Collection PHOTO12: pp. 4–5, 11, 12–3,

14, 15, 16, 21, 25, 38, 39, 49, 57, 60, 64, 70, 71, 75, 81, 96 (2nd col. top), 103.
Collection Rue des Archives: pp. 6, 43.
Roman Polansi, Paris: p. 97 (2nd col.; 3rd col.).

Screen grabs: pp. 28, 85.

Credits

© AMLF: p. 65.
© Archives du 7e Art/DR: pp. 4–5, 11, 12–3, 14, 15, 16, 21, 38, 49, 57, 60, 70, 71, 75, 96 (2nd col.), 103.
© BAC Films: pp. 34–5, 97 (3rd col.).
© Burrill Productions/Columbia Pictures Corporation/StudioCanal/Les Films Alain Sarde/R. P. Productions: pp. 46, 47, 48.
© Carthago Films: pp. 44–5, 96 (4th col. bottom), 97 (1st col. top), 99 (3rd col. middle).
© Columbia Pictures: p. 62.
© Columbia Pictures/Renn Productions: pp. 63, 66–7.

© Compton Films/Tekli British Productions: pp. 74, 96 (3rd col.).
© Elizabeth Brach/Rue des Archives: p. 43.
© Films Polski/Unité de production Kamera: pp. 8, 9, 10, 96 (2nd col.).
© Lodz Films/Films Polski: p. 96 (1st col. bottom).
© MGM: pp. 18, 20, 22–3, 24, 96 (4th col. top).
© NPF: pp. 40–1.
© Paramount Pictures: cover, pp. 2–3, 26–7, 29, 30, 32–3, 36, 42, 50, 52–3, 54–5, 56, inside back cover.
© Photo12/DR: pp. 25, 39, 64.

© Photo12/Jacky Godard: p. 81.
© RP Films: inside front cover, pp. 68–9, 72, 82, 83, 84, 86, 87, 88–9, 97 (4th col.), 101.
© Rue des Archives/AGIP: p. 6.
© Studio Canal/BAC Films: pp. 76–7, 78, 79, 80.
© Warner Bros Ent. Inc.: pp. 58–9, 97 (2nd col.).
© Warner Bros/The Mount Company: p. 97 (1st col. bottom).
© Wild Bunch Distribution: pp. 90, 92, 93, 94–5.

All reasonable efforts have been made to trace the copyright holders of the photographs used in this book. We apologize to anyone that we were unable to reach.

Cover: Mia Farrow in *Rosemary's Baby* (1968).
Inside front cover: Roman Polanski on the set of *The Ghost Writer* (2010).
Inside back cover: Roman Polanski in *The Tenant* (1976).
Opposite page: Roman Polanski with cinematographer Sven Nykvist on the set of *The Tenant* (1976).

Acknowledgments

Thanks to Bill Krohn and Bill Reed.
To the memory of Raymond Durgnat.

Cahiers du cinéma Sarl
65, rue Montmartre
75002 Paris

www.cahiersducinema.com

First published 2012 © 2012 Cahiers du cinéma Sarl

ISBN 978 2 8664 2917 1

Series conceived by Claudine Paquot
Concept designed by Werner Jeker/Les Ateliers du Nord
Designed by Pascaline Richir
Printed in China